TELEPEN
60 0008568 8

KU-512-816

and External Readers | Staff &

FOR RETURN

LEGE

CANCELLED

SAPIENTER PROFICIENS

CANCELLED

LIBRARY

# Antique
# English Furniture

# Antique
# English Furniture

Edward T. Joy

Ward Lock Ltd London

Eaton Hall
College ... CANCELLED ...ary

# ACKNOWLEDGEMENTS

The author and publishers are indebted to the following for the use of illustrative material in this book.

N. Adams, P. Agius, Asprey's, British Museum, Gregory, M. Harris, Hotspur, Jetley, H. W. Keil Ltd, Knight, Mallett, Brian Nicholls of Oakham, Partridge, Perry, Spirk, Temple Williams, Victoria and Albert Museum, Worshipful Company of Goldsmiths.

NOTTINGHAMSHIRE

CANCELLED

3710457

COUNTY LIBRARY

© Edward T. Joy 1972

ISBN 0 7063 1052 7

First published in Great Britain 1972 by Ward Lock Limited, 116 Baker Street, London, W1M 2BB

All Rights Reserved. No part of this publication may be reproduced, stored in a retrieval system, or transmitted, in any form or by any means, electronic, mechanical, photocopying, recording, or otherwise, without the prior permission of the Copyright owner(s).

*Printed and bound by Editorial Fher SA, Bilbao, Spain.*

# Contents

# PART 1

# Traditions of English Furniture Design and Manufacture

Furniture has been used in Britain since early times, but it is only comparatively recently, perhaps within the last two or three centuries, that it became the accepted part of every household. Before that it was the treasured possession of the the well-to-do, and its gradual spread through society is a mark of the general improvement in the standard of living. In this process of development English furniture has acquired a very good reputation for its sound craftsmanship and straightforward design, in which use is made of wood to the best advantage.

Types and styles of furniture change in response to social demands, so that while English craftsmen have freely borrowed foreign constructional techniques and decorative styles, they have always adapted them skilfully to the needs and tastes of the English. Similarly, since there has always been European free trade in furniture designs, English furniture has been in great demand abroad and, indeed, over the last three hundred years, England has exported her furniture in increasing quantities to all parts of the world. This is something worth underlining, for too much attention has been concentrated on the debt which English craftsmanship has owed to foreign influences with little regard for the way—and extent—foreigners have been influenced by English furniture.

During the Middle Ages, from about 1100 to 1500, the small amount of furniture in existence belonged mostly to the wealthier classes—royalty, the aristocracy and churchmen—and was taken with them when they visited the palaces, castles and manor houses on their estates. Their furniture thus had to be portable and consisted mainly of chests (which were very useful for storage), benches, stools and trestle tables, which could easily be stacked and transported. To this day the word for furniture in many European languages can be translated as 'movables'. Chairs were rare and enjoyed enormous status since they were reserved for persons of distinction, subordinates had to make do with benches and stools. The dignity accorded to the chair can be seen in obvious examples such as a royal throne or a bishop's seat. The latter, the *cathedra*, (the Greek word for throne) gives its name to the cathedral, the principal church of the diocese. Today in the British House of Commons all the members, even those in the Cabinet, sit on benches while the only chair is reserved for the Speaker who controls parliamentary debates. There were three main types of medieval chairs: the chair of state, of which the Coronation Chair in Westminster Abbey is an excellent example, the 'X-' (or cross-) frame or folding chair, and the turned (or 'thrown') chair, in which the turned structural members were socketed into the seat and into one another for strength.

Medieval 'travelling' furniture inevitably suffered hard usage. At first it was made by a carpenter, though more refined work was produced by a turner and carver. For decoration, furniture was painted or carved. The carver, who was mainly employed on ecclesiastical woodwork, naturally decorated chests and chairs of state with pointed arches, crockets and leaf ornament which he carved on screens and bench ends. Occasionally, simple attempts at roundels and similar forms ('chip carving') could be found.

In the fifteenth century there were decided improvements in both design and construction. The rising class of rich wool merchants and traders demanded comfort in a society which was becoming more settled. This was supplied by the improved construction of panel and frame, the work of the joiner which led to better-made, more compact and attractively proportioned furniture. 'Joined' furniture, so called because it employed the mortise and tenon joint, was, like the panelling on the walls of the room in which it stood, meant to stay in one place. Thus joined tables began to replace trestle tables and the chest, still an important piece, was put in a prominent position in the house. Chest panels were often carved with 'linenfold' decoration which, like the panel and frame technique itself, reached England from Flanders. Chairs were also built up in panels to establish the traditional framework with square or rectangular backs (the 'panel-back'), the production of which remained the special province of the joiner for over two centuries. Various kinds of small tables stood about the house, including cupboards, which were not enclosed pieces but literally cupboards or side tables ('board' being the old word for table).

Enclosed spaces were known as 'aumbries' and were sometimes found as part of a larger piece of furniture. Presses were larger storage pieces for clothes. With the growth of towns, crafts guilds attained their greatest influence and increasing specialisation marked the work of carpenters, joiners, turners and cofferers. The last named were for a time the aristocrats of furniture-makers, and the first to appear as royal craftsmen. Their function was to make fine coffers, chests and standards, and to cover them with rich fabric materials which they also applied to such pieces as chairs of state.

Throughout this period the wood chiefly used for furniture was oak. Indeed 'the age of oak' has become the term used to refer to the period in furniture-making from earliest times until about 1660.

The sixteenth century—the Tudor Period—saw more significant changes. The internal peace established by the strong Tudor monarchy, and the Dissolution of the Monasteries (1536–39), with the consequent creation of a new landowning class through the sales of the great monastic estates, encouraged the building of large new houses (the famous 'prodigy' houses) which emphasised comfort rather than defence. Like all *nouveaux-riches*, these landowners went in for much ostentatious display, and new types of furniture, or old types adapted for up-to-date usage, were eagerly taken up and flamboyantly decorated.

In addition to panel-back chairs of established design, a lighter type, the 'caquetoire' or 'conversation' chair (from the French *caqueter*, to gossip) appeared in many houses. It was

The late Tudor bedstead had its tester supported on a solid panelled headboard and two foot posts. This bed, dated 1585, is of walnut and has the characteristic constructional and decorative features of panelling, turned posts, carving and inlay with box and holly.

14

obviously intended to be easily moved about, probably for ladies' use. 'Draw-tables', with two extendable leaves beneath the top, came into use with the development of separate dining rooms for the family. Landowners gradually abandoned the medieval custom of having their meals with their retainers in the Great Hall, the old centre of communal life in palaces, castles and manor houses. While most cupboards retained their old function as side tables, some were beginning to be enclosed with doors. 'Livery' cupboards, for instance, had pierced doors to provide ventilation for their stores of food. Beds, which had formerly been frameworks of wood covered with expensive materials, beneath a canopy of rich hangings suspended from the ceiling, now acquired elaborate headboards and posts to support the 'tester' or canopy.

These changes in the early Tudor Period might have been much more far-reaching if England had been in closer touch with the Italian Renaissance and its revival of interest in classical design and decoration. But the Reformation under Henry VIII (1509–47), making its effects felt first in the 1530s, cut England from direct contact with Italy. Her closest cultural ties were with the Protestant countries of the Netherlands and Germany. From these sources came an ornate version of the new classicism which affected English furniture for the rest of the century. The influence was most noticeable in Elizabeth I's reign (1558–1603), because these Protestant countries were pioneers in the new art of printing and exported to England printed pattern books of furniture designs which were readily adopted by English craftsmen.

The most important foreign designer was Vredeman de Vries (1527–1604), a Fleming, whose influence can be detected in late Tudor and Jacobean furniture. Before the Reformation there had been some traces of classical Renaissance influence on English furniture. This manifested itself in 'Romayne' work—carved profiles set within roundels—and in decorative motifs such as the acanthus leaf, vases and Ionic capitals, all of which were freely mixed with Gothic carving and linenfold.

After about 1550, however, came the vogue for grotesque

'bulbs' which were built up on table legs and bed posts, strapwork, composed of interlaced geometric patterns and arabesques, and inlay in chequered and floral designs. The florid character of some of these decorative forms clearly appealed to the national love of display encouraged by exuberant self-confidence of the times, heightened by the defeat of the Spanish Armada in 1588.

The Elizabethan Age also witnessed a radical change in the design of houses, both externally and internally. Often built in the shape of an 'H' or half 'H' (Montacute House, Somerset, 1580–1601, is a good example of the latter), these 'extrovert' houses looked out on to pleasant gardens and were no longer inward-looking within a defensive moat. Inside, the Great Hall was replaced by a smaller great chamber, a separate dining room, more private rooms and, biggest innovation of all, the long gallery, running the whole length of the house in the upper storey. Chairs retained their symbolic status and were still comparatively scarce. Inventories of royal palaces and of a few great houses, taken when their owners died, reveal that wealthy men had some magnificently upholstered chairs, the covering being obviously worth a great deal more than the woodwork. Unfortunately, such inventories contain insufficient evidence to enable us to judge how many of these elaborate chairs were made by foreign craftsmen and how many by Englishmen. In Winchester Cathedral there still is an oak X-frame chair which was originally covered with gilt nails and traditionally used by Queen Mary Tudor at her wedding to Philip II of Spain in 1554. It is a solitary survivor of this grand type of chair and was almost certainly the work of an English cofferer.

The late Tudor prestige piece, apart from the chair of state, was the 'court' cupboard, a three-tiered open sideboard used to display the family plate on ceremonial occasions. These pieces were still cupboards in the old sense, but some had an enclosed compartment in the middle shelf while larger examples had two stages, the lower stage being enclosed by doors (with shelves inside), the upper having a recessed cupboard.

A new type of chair without arms, known at the time as a 'back stool', made its appearance in the second half of the sixteenth century. It may well have been made for the members of the family sitting round the now centrally sited dining table. They no longer had a wall to rest their backs against, as was the case when they took their meals on the dais in the great hall. Shortly after 1600 a broader version of the back stool, with upholstered seat and back, was made; this type has been given the modern name of 'farthingale' chair. While one must be cautious about the validity of such modern terms, the chair's wider dimensions do seem to have been designed to accommodate ladies wearing the fashionable hooped farthingale dress. Stools were still the commonest seats and were made *en suite* with chairs. After about 1550 'joined' stools came into fashion, with four turned legs linked to a rail beneath the seat and connected by stretchers just above floor level. There was also a revival of folding chairs which have been given the name of 'Glastonbury' chairs. These demonstrated the increasing demand for portable furniture of which another example was the 'gate-leg' table with extendable flaps.

In general, the types of furniture and their decorative features which had emerged by the end of the Tudor Period continued under the early Stuarts until about 1650. In some ways this was a disappointingly uncreative period in the development of English furniture. Charles I (1625–49) was fully alive to the important cultural movements on the Continent, movements which served to show up the relative backwardness of the arts and crafts in England. He made determined efforts to bring the country up-to-date by establishing a magnificent collection of pictures, and encouraging the royal architect, Inigo Jones, who introduced neo-classical Palladian-style architecture into England. But political events—Charles's quarrel with Parliament, the Civil War and Cromwell's republican régime marked by Puritan austerity—contrived to halt these promising developments in the arts, architecture and interior decoration. In spite of all this there was, however, some progress in furniture design. The exuberance of Tudor decoration largely disappeared. The great 'bulbs', for example, gave way to thinner and more graceful turned members. Carved decoration employed more classical motifs. It was a great age for English needlework, since the ladies of the household often upholstered their seat furniture with needlework using coloured wools on a canvas base—a cheap and durable material. The chest of drawers in a rudimentary form made its appearance, developing the 'tills' or small drawers which had been fitted into some furniture since Tudor times, and improving on the 'mule' chest, with its single bottom drawer, which was already in use. Smaller houses contained a sturdy type of chair given the name of the 'Yorkshire and Derbyshire' chair because of its connection with those areas. Its chief feature was the construction of the back—either an open arcade between two rails joined by turned balusters, or two broad hoops decorated with carving.

The year 1660, the year of the Restoration of Charles II to the throne, opened a completely new era in English furniture history. Indeed, many historians regard this year as the real beginning of English furniture, for there were now the closest possible links with all the latest continental developments in design, decoration and styles of furniture. These influences were absorbed with such remarkable speed by English furniture craftsmen that within a generation or so the quality of their work was beginning to match that of the best of their foreign rivals. Charles II and his Court set the fashion in luxurious living and their example was readily followed throughout the country, not only by the landed aristocracy but also by the prosperous commercial classes who were taking full advantage of the rapid expansion of overseas trade. The reaction against Cromwell's Puritanism naturally encouraged this swing towards a more comfortable mode of life. The Great Fire of London in 1666, happening so soon after the Restoration, turned out to be a boon to English craftsmen, for the capital had to be largely rebuilt and refurnished. The new type of brick houses, with their large sash windows, well-proportioned rooms and light-coloured walls, required up-to-date, compact, attractive furniture. Foreign craftsmen, especially French and Dutch, came to London to teach their skills to English apprentices. The age produced new techniques and decoration, a fashionable new timber, walnut, and a new class of highly skilled craftsmen. As the age of oak gave way to the age of walnut, so the joiner gave way to the cabinet-maker as the principal craftsman in furniture.

The cabinet-maker acquired his title from his ability to produce the new prestige piece, the cabinet, and to decorate it with veneers, marquetry and parquetry. Cabinets were at first supported on stands; their folding doors enclosed numerous small drawers in which their wealthy owners kept their collections of 'curiosities', the small valuable objects such as coins, jewels and medals which could be gathered up quickly in case of emergency.

The chairs of Charles II's reign (1660–85) are distinguished for their tall backs and elaborate decoration, which was natural enough in the first flush of reaction against Puritanism. Wide, flat, carved and pierced walnut frames enclosing panels of cane made up the backs, surmounted by an ornate cresting rail which often matched the decoration of the flat stretcher between the front legs. The latter, like the arms and arm supports, were scrolled. Spiral turned uprights and stretchers added their final touches of flamboyancy. 'Day-beds', or couches, already in use before 1660, were decorated in the same way as chairs. Wing armchairs, so called from the extending 'ear-pieces' to exclude draughts, were now found in private rooms and their well-upholstered seats, arms and backs illustrate the growing search for comfort.

As the example of the cabinet shows, it was now fashionable to rest case furniture of all kinds on stands, a technique borrowed from continental practice. This was done with chests of drawers and writing cabinets or 'scrutores'. The latter were copied directly from French models and had a large fall-front which was let down to provide a writing surface. After the Great Fire of London there was a decided increase in the making of furniture intended for writing. Many City merchants had moved out into the suburbs and

19

needed writing furniture in their new homes, and the much
improved postal services in Britain since the establishment of
the General Letter Office in 1661 both reflected and encouraged the growing habit of letter-writing.

It was not only Europe that contributed so much to
English furniture styles. Through the East India Company,
England now came under the spell of strange new materials
and decorative ideas from India and the Far East. Oriental
lacquer, with its marvellously bright colours and exotic
scenes, was imported in increasing quantities, sometimes as
furniture, especially cabinets, sometimes as panels and
screens which were used as veneers on English furniture.
English merchants even sent models of English furniture to the
East in the Company's ships to be copied and lacquered by
Eastern craftsmen, then re-imported, a lengthy but lucrative
business. Attempts were made to manufacture an English

The interior of the japanned cabinet (page 101) continues the exterior
decoration which is based on designs in Stalker & Parker's *Treatise of
Japanning*, 1688.

form of lacquer, a home-made substitute known as 'japan'. This imitative work was much encouraged by the publication of a manual in 1688 under the title of *A Treatise of Japanning and Varnishing* by Stalker and Parker. But japanning never matched the brilliancy or durability of the original. English japanners, however, did succeed in persuading Parliament in 1701 to impose crippling import duties on lacquer, leaving the home market largely free for their own products. Meanwhile, many rich late Stuart households had acquired their lacquered cabinets, with richly chased metal hinges and back plates, and, following the prevailing custom, they were usually placed on ornate gilded or silvered stands specially made for them.

The eighteenth century was a distinguished period for English science. Under Sir Isaac Newton's leadership modern science—as we know it—was established in Europe. In the domestic sphere this was seen in the vastly improved methods of time-keeping. English clockmakers entered on their golden age, their products being unmatched throughout the world for accuracy and beauty. The 'long-case' clock, more familiarly known as the grandfather clock, had a long pendulum attached to its weight-driven mechanism, all enclosed in a finely decorated case. The table or bracket clock had a handle for carrying it about the house. Walnut veneers, marquetry and parquetry, lacquer and japanning were all found as decoration on clocks. Among the many distinguished makers of the time Thomas Tompion stands supreme.

In the last two Stuart reigns, those of William and Mary (1689–1702) and Anne (1702–14), a new wave of foreign influence was felt. William of Orange brought cabinet-makers and designers over from Holland with him, including the Huguenot Daniel Marot. Also the Revocation of the Edict of Nantes in 1685 drove many French Huguenots, outstanding craftsmen among them, to seek the freedom and religious toleration of England. Through them English craftsmen were introduced directly to the very latest developments at the court of Louis XIV. A sprinkling of foreign names among the royal craftsmen at the English court—Pelletier and Jensen, for instance, as well as Marot—shows how much the royal palaces and through them the great aristocratic houses, benefited from this influence.

After 1690 chairs shed their fancy Carolean trimmings. Those of the William and Mary period had graceful baluster uprights crowned by a cresting rail. This was put on and not between the uprights, thus giving them an extraordinarily tall appearance. Baluster turned legs also replaced the former curved ones. Chair backs were filled with upholstery whenever cane was not employed. Under Marot's influence some chairs had the whole filling of their backs composed of carved and pierced wood. Then, just before 1700, the 'curvilinear' chair brought a totally new conception into English chair design. The chair back at last began to lose its square or rectangular framework and took on curved uprights with a central solid splat which was shaped in attractive vase or urn forms, and was also 'bended' to make a hollow for the sitter's shoulders. In addition, the 'cabriole' leg, wide at the knee for strength, but curving down to slender ankle and hoof, club or claw-and-ball foot, completed the display of controlled curves which distinguished this new type of chair. The carved decoration of acanthus and shells on the knees, cresting rail and front seat rail, and the walnut veneers on the seat rails and on the 'bended' splat—all found on the best examples of these chairs—clearly demonstrate the remarkable skill of English craftsmen.

Simple dignity was the great feature of the furniture of this later walnut period. Cabinets, scrutores and chests of drawers were no longer supported on stands but stood either on chests of drawers for greater stability—hence the double chest of drawers, the chest on chest, or 'tallboy'—or rested on the floor. Great attention was paid to good proportions and functionalism. The scrutore, for instance, was in vogue for some time until the inconvenience of its large fall-front and the lack of space in its interior led to its gradual replacement by the 'bureau'. The latter had a handy sloping top and space behind it into which papers could be pushed when the top was closed. By the time of Anne's reign both chests of drawers

The desk was another library feature. This pedestal type shown here has three drawers in the frieze, three in one pedestal and twelve (marked alphabetically) in the other. It was probably made c. 1760.

and bureaux (which are chests of drawers with a sloping writing top) acquired their familiar present-day forms.

A composite piece, the bureau-bookcase, at that time known as a 'desk and bookcase', was also being produced. The upper doors were usually fronted with looking-glass plates and their tops, though sometimes finished off with a straight cornice, were given imposing arched domes or a variety of broken pediments, straight, curved or 'swan-neck', with a central plinth to support a classical urn or shield. At ground level such pieces had at first rested on ball or bun feet, but these were replaced about 1700 by the well-designed shapely bracket feet.

Much case furniture was of narrow width, intended to stand against the 'pier' (the wall space between windows) in order to get light from both sides. More mirrors on the walls, in tall, narrow, flat frames, sometimes with a shell carved on their shaped crests, added to rooms a brightness never experienced before. Mirror glass, however, was still expensive, even though its price had fallen when its manufacture had begun in England about 1670 and it no longer had to be imported from abroad. A charming small mirror, the dressing glass, a swing mirror framed above a stand with miniature drawers for toilet articles, was fashionable in Anne's reign. It usually stood on a dressing table which took the form of pedestals with drawers flanking a knee-hole recess, or of a table with drawers resting on cabriole legs.

With the development of furniture of smaller scale the heavy joined table went out of fashion. It was altogether too big and clumsy for the new-style rooms. For eating rooms, gate-leg tables were much more convenient, since they could be set up for a meal then closed and moved to the wall and used as side tables. A set of three such tables, two of semi-circular shape and one rectangular, was particularly useful for extending into one long table. The national craze for card playing led to the production of the first tables specially designed for this pastime. In the reign of William and Mary these tables had hinged oval or circular tops unfolding to rest on gate-legs. In the following reign the vogue was for rectangular folding tops on four legs, one of which, hinged to the rail, swung out for support. The corners were rounded for candlesticks, and the baize-covered tops contained four sunken wells for coins or gaming-counters. Much was made of the attractiveness of small tables as well as of their obvious usefulness. A fashionable grouping of the period was the 'table, glass and stands', a combination of a side table standing against the wall beneath a looking glass and, at each side, a candle stand.

The Georgian Period, from the accession of George I in 1714 till the death of George IV in 1830, is justly celebrated as the 'golden age' of English cabinet-making. One reason for its success lay in the peculiarly intimate relationship between patron, designer and craftsman. Standards of taste were conditioned by the needs of the cultured upper classes, who, reared in a thorough knowledge of the classics at school and university, completed their education in a very practical way by making the 'grand tour'. This sometimes lasted three or four years, the purpose being to study at first hand the art and architecture of classical antiquity and of the Renaissance. A competent working knowledge of architecture, the arts and crafts was expected of every gentleman. The growing wealth of the country, from agriculture, overseas trade and industry, provided the ruling class with the means to indulge their tastes.

Professional architects now included furniture as an essential part of their designs. Craftsmen reached the peak of hand skills and were themselves trained as designers, some of them showing remarkable versatility of invention. At their command was a wealth of superb materials. The world was combed for exotic timbers while at home a choice assortment of textiles for upholstery and furnishings was now available, including the varied products of the Huguenot silk weavers who had settled in Spitalfields, London, after 1685. London was, in fact, the chief furniture centre. It attracted the best craftsmen and catered for the Court, the aristocracy and the landed gentry who made their seasonal visits to the capital to keep abreast of latest fashions. These fashions changed with amazing rapidity as artists, designers and craftsmen applied their minds to new ideas and schemes, and taste swung from one direction to another. The styles were popularised by a series of famous pattern books issued by craftsmen-designers.

The Georgian Period is epitomised by mahogany, a timber which began to reach England from the West Indies in increasing quantities in the second quarter of the century as a result of the abolition in 1721 of the heavy duties on its import. The cabinet-makers could not have found a better timber for their skill; it had fine figure and colour, could be carved crisply or used as a veneer, was immensely strong, and (unlike walnut) was impervious to worm. It could also be obtained in the wide planks needed for table tops and cup-board doors. At first the heavy close-grained 'Spanish' wood from San Domingo and Jamaica (much of it from this British island was smuggled from the Spanish colonies) was in fashion. Later, after 1750, varieties from Honduras and Cuba came on the market, and particularly favoured were the famous Cuban figures such as curls and feathers.

While mahogany was gradually superseding walnut as the fashionable wood, there was a swing away from the studied simplicity of design which characterised Anne's reign. The remarkable carving qualities of mahogany led to the 'lion period', so called from the prevalence of lion's paws, manes and masks carved on cabriole legs. Other typical carved ornaments were shells, cabochons and satyr masks, with much acanthus foliage on table frames. Eagles' heads were found as terminal decoration on chair arms. Chairs themselves had wider seats and splayed arms to accommodate the wide costume worn by both men and women, and splats were now pierced. The tendency towards more ornate furniture reached its apogee under the influence of William Kent (1685–1748), the first English architect to treat furniture as an integral part of his interiors. It was through his patron, the Earl of Burlington, himself an architectural designer, that Kent brought about a revival of Palladian-style architecture. For his carefully formal interiors he designed baroque furniture. Grand side tables, profusely carved with swags, human masks, lion heads and acanthus, either gilded or of mahogany parcel gilt, were perhaps most typical of the furniture which he designed. Similar forms of ornament could be found on his chairs, pier glasses, chests, bookcases, pedestals and 'console' tables. The last named, another innovation from France, rested on a gilt spread eagle or on two brackets against the wall. Friezes of tables and frames of chairs were carved with the Greek key or Vitruvian scroll. Although Kent's designs mark a distinct phase in English furniture, outside upper class circles they seem to have done little more than stimulate an architectural approach to case furniture, and already in Kent's lifetime his furniture was

This mirror of c. 1765, with gilt frame in asymmetrical rococo taste, lacks the finesse of the delicately carved ornament associated with *Director* mirrors.

being criticised as too monumental.

The inevitable reaction came in the 1750s. It was marked by the 'rococo', a revolt against classical formality by a swing to lively, delicate, asymmetrical themes typified by 'C' and 'S' scrolls and serpentine lines. It also produced the most famous of all English cabinet-makers, Thomas Chippendale (1718–79), whose version of rococo furniture, a skilful English interpretation of a style born and developed in France, has given his name to the mid-century taste which has become known all over the world. The Yorkshire-born Chippendale, who came to London to make his fortune, achieved fame in 1754 when he published *The Gentleman and Cabinet-Maker's Director*, the first pattern book to be completely devoted to furniture designs. In addition to rococo, Chippendale also presented furniture in Chinese and Gothic styles. The book, intended for prospective purchasers as well as for craftsmen, was a distinct success, and was re-issued in 1755 and again, much enlarged, in 1762.

Chippendale's rococo designs depended largely on delicate carving carried out in mahogany. His famous chairs best illustrate this. Under a cresting rail of 'cupid's bow' form, the splat was now carved and pierced in daring scrolls which in some examples resembled festoons of ribbons. The uprights curved gently upwards and outwards, and the cabriole leg now achieved a very delicate form, ending, not on a claw-and-ball foot, but on a 'French scroll' (turned outward) or 'knurl foot' (curved inward). 'Commodes', the ornamental chests of drawers which may be considered the prestige pieces of the Georgian period, had serpentine fronts and the same kind of carved ornament that the chairs had. Other favourite pieces for this full rococo treatment were console tables and mirror frames, the latter demonstrating perhaps better than any other piece of furniture the fashionable delight in asymmetrical ornament.

The *Director* designs excelled in two particular branches of furniture to which England could claim to have made a special contribution—for the library, and for tea-drinking. The 'break-front' bookcase, with projecting central section,

was treated in classical form or with rococo ornament on the framework and cornice; similar carving was found on pedestal library tables, as on the famous example supplied by Chippendale himself to Nostell Priory, Yorkshire. In tea furniture the delicacy of the rococo was seen at its best. Tea-time was an interim meal for which the appropriate furniture was carried to the centre of the room, then carried away. Hence the essential lightness of urn stands, tea caddy stands and tea tables. The latter, also called 'china' tables, were often found in 'pillar and claw form', on a tripod on three feet, with a circular top ringed with a miniature fretted gallery or with a scalloped ('piecrust') edging.

In adapting Chinese designs for furniture, Chippendale used geometric frets ('Chinese railings') as low relief carving on chair and table legs (which in this style were straight and not cabriole), or as fretted galleries on tables and on cabinet furniture. This geometric patterning formed a happy contrast with the curves of the rococo, but there were also many Chinese motifs of small scale—including pagodas, mandarins, long-necked birds, dragons, bullrushes and bells, freely mixed with flowing foliage. It is a measure of Chippendale's talent that all blended very successfully with the general rococo fashion. So too with Gothic designs. Crockets, pinnacles and pointed arches were all delicately carved to decorate furniture in Gothic rooms, a fashion set by Horace Walpole's Gothic villa at Strawberry Hill, Twickenham.

Chippendale's name has been given, and very rightly, to his translation of the rococo, and is universally used as the label of his style. However, very little furniture in the *Director* style can be unequivocally assigned to Chippendale's work-shop. Where there is clear documentary evidence, as in the case of the Nostell Priory library table, for Chippendale's bills are preserved in the house, there is no case for argument. But short of this conclusive proof there is little ground for attribution. Too often in the past Chippendale pieces have been sold to customers who believed that Chippendale made them. Nobody now should be so misled. The very success of the *Director* indicated that it was being widely used by cabinet-makers to work from, and many of them could quite easily match anything produced by Chippendale's firm. Chippendale never obtained a royal appointment, though he served people of distinction and worked in St. Martin's Lane, London, the principal cabinet-making centre of London. His neighbour, William Vile, a royal cabinet-maker, made furniture in the *Director* taste which surpassed the known work by Chippendale in the same period. Vile's name, like those of his partner, John Cobb, and of other distinguished contemporaries, including Benjamin Goodison, William France, John Bradburn, and the partners Ince and Mayhew, has been obscured until recently by the fame of the *Director*, though their emergence into the light should not detract, as some critics have insisted, from the general worth of Chippendale's achievement.

Meanwhile the Chippendale style was spreading throughout the world. In Europe, from Russia in the north to Venice in the south, from Norway to Spain and Portugal and east to Turkey, English furniture was in great demand. Many surviving pieces of this mid-century trade can be seen today in foreign museums alongside adaptations made by native cabinet-makers. The style was eagerly followed in the American colonies where craftsmen, reared in the English tradition, made their own versions, sometimes from imported models. The thriving seaports on the eastern coast frequently imported cargoes of furniture from London, and their newspapers, when announcing these newly-arrived goods, also advertised shops whose cabinet-makers and upholsterers had the distinction of being trained in England. In Europe, foreign craftsmen of special skill, like Georg Haupt, the Swede, and Abraham Roentgen, the German, came to London to complete their training. Early in this century Dutch cabinet-makers gained full membership of their guild by submitting an 'English cabinet' as their masterpiece, while Swedish, Danish and German craftsmen were found adopting the title of 'English cabinet-maker' or 'chair-maker' as marks of distinction.

The established excellence of fashionable English furniture

31

should not obscure the fine quality of the more homely 'country' pieces which were made by provincial joiners and carpenters. Increasing attention is now being paid to this vernacular furniture, springing from basic social needs and firmly rooted in tradition, eschewing unnecessary decoration and achieving an attractive and innate simplicity of design. Unfortunately, it is just this type of furniture which tends to be lost in the process of time, though in one way, in the ease with which it can be repeated and replaced, its fundamental pattern can survive. An outstanding example of the longevity of the vernacular style is the 'Windsor' chair. Made of 'sticks' socketed in the seat to form a back beneath a fan-shaped rail or, after about 1750, a hoop or bent bow, and with turned legs and stretchers, the Windsor was the established cottage chair which has also made its home in America since the earliest days of the Colonial period. Its name remains a mystery, for there is no evidence to connect it specifically with Windsor; it was in fact known throughout England as the 'stick-back'. Another long-established vernacular chair is the 'ladder-back', of which a fashionable version was made in Chippendale's time, and again in the Arts and Crafts Movement of the later nineteenth century, when there was a revival of interest in cottage crafts. Both types of chair made belated concessions to fashionable taste by incorporating decorative mannerisms or structural changes (such as the cabriole leg on Windsor chairs) to try to keep up-to-date.

From symmetry to asymmetry, then back to symmetry; so the changes in fashion followed each other. In the mid-1760s the scrolls and swirls of the rococo had had their day, and classicism returned to favour guided by the masterly hand of Robert Adam (1728–92), the great Scottish architect and designer. Adam, however, did not revive the monumental grandeur of the 'baroque', but picked up from the rococo a lightness which he applied to his neo-classicism. Hence the characteristic vocabulary of festoons of husks, vases, paterae, honeysuckle, rams' heads, medallions and the like, based firmly on classical precedents but executed with a highly individual delicacy.

Adam designed some but by no means all the furniture in his houses. This is contrary to the long-accepted view that he designed all the contents to achieve uniformity. Recent research shows that he designed furniture to stand against the wall—mirrors, side tables, sideboards, stands of various kinds and, occasionally, chairs—which he regarded as a normal part of the room's decoration. But all other pieces were designed by cabinet-makers called in for the purpose, including Chippendale whose best work was done, not in his own *Director* style, but in this new post-1765 classicism. To execute designs in the Adam style involved a radical re-appraisal of decorative media. While there was some excellent carved work, it was fashionable to show neo-classical ornament in marquetry, which now underwent a remarkable revival. Light-coloured woods, of which satinwood was the most important, were in demand, and against their background a large variety of woods set out the classical motifs with consummate skill, often on awkwardly shaped surfaces, such as the French *bombé*. Some of the greatest masterpieces of English cabinet-making were produced at this time, rivalling the best that France could make. They include Linnell's furniture at Osterley, Cobb's at Stourhead and above all, Chippendale's at Harewood House, where his famous *Diana and Minerva* commode was supplied in 1773 at a cost of £86.

English neo-classical chair design entered another great pioneering phase. Chairs for the first time acquired round and oval backs, and these soon developed into a number of interesting new forms, including 'heart-' and 'shield-backs'. Legs on all kinds of furniture were straight and tapered, either round or square in section, and sometimes splaying outwards, with or without stretchers. Adam's personal influence is seen in his 'sideboards', a fine grouping of a side table flanked by a pair of pedestal cupboards each supporting a classical urn. In time this became a smaller piece familiar in modern dining rooms, the flanking cupboards being placed beneath the table to save space.

Adam's neo-classical designs, which were executed for a

circle of wealthy clients, were popularised by George Hepplewhite whose *Cabinet-Maker and Upholsterer's Guide* of 1788 is the second of the famous trilogy of Georgian pattern books. But unlike Chippendale, Hepplewhite was an obscure cabinet-maker, of Cripplegate, London, and no furniture from his shop has ever been identified. In fact, he died two years before the appearance of his *Guide* which seems to have been published by his widow. Nevertheless, Hepplewhite is a well-deserved label for the elegant furniture of excellent proportions which was designed for middle-class homes and was in general use in the last quarter of the eighteenth century. Hepplewhite's furniture was intended to be made in mahogany or satinwood, or painted and japanned. The *Guide* was re-issued in 1789 and in revised form in 1794.

Among Hepplewhite's chair designs, the most famous is the 'shield-back' which, like the oval and heart shapes which he also sponsored, he took over from the established neo-classical repertoire, but did not himself originate. He may, however, have been the first to apply to chairs the Prince of Wales's feathers, which had already been used to decorate other pieces of furniture. These feathers made a very attractive filling for his shield-backs, but were only part of the many motifs—foliage, draperies, wheat-ears, honeysuckle, vases and husks—which were now employed. For bedroom chairs the *Guide* recommended the "new and very elegant fashion" of japanning and when this decoration was used, the lighter framework, usually of beech and a cane seat, added much to their charm. As a rule chair legs followed the neo-classical precedent of being straight and tapered and ending on 'plinth' (or spade) feet, without stretchers.

It was Hepplewhite who made the small sideboard fashionable, reduced in scale from Adam's monumental composition. From about 1780 bow-fronted sideboards, sometimes with four legs at the front and two at the back, sometimes with four legs only, came into production, and a little later a 'tambour' front was added in some examples beneath the front drawer. These pieces are very much in demand today because they make such an elegant addition to a modern

Neo-classical furniture conformed to the general decoration of rooms, and side tables were vital adjuncts to the delicate plasterwork and painted decoration of the wall. This side table, of c. 1775, shows typical ornament in the carved, gilded and tapered legs and the painted festoons of husks and paterae on the frieze.

dining room. Equally attractive are Hepplewhite's chests of drawers. When these are straight-fronted, solid mahogany is used, or figured mahogany veneered on pine, oak or sometimes on Honduras mahogany. Serpentine or bow-fronted chests employed mahogany veneer on a pine carcase. Instead of a plinth for a support, the corners of the chest were brought down to the floor in French fashion to outward-curving feet, and to continue the design of gentle curves an apron piece was carried across the bottom of the frame.

Elegant small tables in many varieties and for many uses were given much attention in the *Guide*. The 'Pembroke' table, fashionable after about 1765, with flaps of circular, serpentine or rectangular shape, standing on square or round tapering legs, has always been acknowledged as one of the most graceful small tables ever made in England. The opened flaps were supported on wooden brackets attached by wooden hinges to the framework. Their tops were sometimes decorated with a small classical or shell design. Graceful touches were everywhere apparent—in the glazing bars, for example, of larger pieces such as bureau-bookcases and break-front library bookcases, and in the turned and reeded bedposts, carved with classical designs.

The prevailing tendency towards lightness reached its peak at the end of the century in the designs of Thomas Sheraton (1751–1806) who completed the great trilogy of furniture patterns with his *Cabinet-Maker's and Upholsterer's Drawing Book*, published in parts between 1791 and 1794. Sheraton remains a curious character. So far as we know, he did not keep a shop, and not a single piece of furniture can definitely be assigned to him. He died in poverty after eking out a miserable existence as a drawing master. Yet his designs, presented with admirable technical assurance, and accompanied by full notes, caught the full flavour of the unsurpassed excellence of late Georgian cabinet-making. His work is of special significance today as he lived at a turning point in furniture history, when the Industrial Revolution was beginning to make its influence felt in English social life and long-accepted traditional ideas were under challenge. Sheraton was keenly aware of these changes, as his designs clearly show.

By the time of Adam's death in 1792 his neo-classicism was already being criticised as too trifling and too personal an interpretation of classical forms; there was a decided swing towards stricter classical rules. Archaeology had become fashionable among scholars and was yielding much accurate information about the furniture of the ancient world. It was, as a result of this knowledge, possible to make exact copies of the furniture of the ancient Egyptians, Greeks and Romans. The emphasis was now on straight lines, in sharp contrast to the curves that had been fashionable since Chippendale's time. Thus Sheraton's chairs had square or rectangular backs, and it was significant that the third edition of Hepplewhite's *Guide* (1794) freely revised its chair designs to include a number in these new forms.

Sheraton lived during a population explosion, and in the days before adequate transport facilities could promote the expansion of cities into suburbs. Consequently the centres of cities, and above all of London, became very crowded and even the well-to-do began to feel the pressure on their living space. Sheraton's response to these changes was to design compact, portable and multi-purpose furniture which could save space. Here he called to his aid the prevalent interest in mechanical devices.

The publication of the *Drawing Book* coincided with the outbreak of war with France in 1793, destined to last, with one short break, until 1815. The simplicity of Sheraton's designs was enhanced by the need for economy which the war imposed. Carving and marquetry became too expensive. It was much cheaper to employ painting or japanning (especially as these were best done on beech, a cheap native wood), and to adopt a simple method of inlay ('stringing') in ebonised wood or brass. Brass indeed was to become a very much favoured material, as it could be used in many ways and was both durable and cheap.

To some critics, Sheraton's furniture is too fragile. This criticism perhaps misses the point of the pressing need for compact furniture and of the kind which could be easily moved about. Hence many of the small tables which appear among Sheraton's designs, for meals, the toilet, writing, needlework and recreation, often combined two or more of these functions in one piece. A writing table would be fitted with an adjustable stand for reading and with a movable screen at the back to protect the sitter from the heat of the fire. The well-known 'Harlequin Pembroke' table had an interior nest of drawers equipped for writing which rose from within the table when one of the flaps was raised, but by the turn of a key the mechanism could be made inoperative and both flaps could be raised and the surface kept clear. Chairs had varied and highly original arrangements of bars in their generally square backs. Their lightness was accentuated in many cases by cane seats, tapered and reeded legs and arms sweeping upwards to form the side seat rails which joined the back near the top. Case furniture mainly followed the trends established by Hepplewhite, with added touches of lightness, but the innovations of the time included roll-top or cylinder covers, sliding to open and shut, on bureaux and bureau-bookcases.

Like Hepplewhite, Sheraton designed for the middle classes, but in doing so he also skillfully interpreted the major changes in style which were influencing the furniture of the upper classes—the changes to which the modern name of 'Regency' has been given. The Regency was in effect the last great phase of classicism, interpreted in the precise archaeological sense, which has already been noted. The main influence, once more, was France, where the fashionable cabinet-makers had been experimenting with the new classicism since just prior to the outbreak of the French Revolution in 1789. Their pioneer work was eagerly taken up by George, Prince of Wales, in 1783, when he came of age and was granted Carlton House as his official residence. The Prince surrounded himself with influential Whig friends and adopted a pro-French attitude to spite his father, George III, well-known for his Tory, anti-French views. Much French furniture was bought through agents to re-furnish Carlton House and the houses which were built or modernised by the Whig coterie. French craftsmen were also employed to carry out the appropriate interior decoration under the general direction of the architect Henry Holland, a keen supporter of this new classical purity. After 1789 more outstanding French furniture came to England, bought cheaply at the sales of the contents of aristocratic homes, or purchased from the aristocrats themselves, a number of whom managed to get away to England with some of their possessions. Thus before the out-

38

break of war with France in 1793, England was in the closest possible touch with the latest developments in French furniture design.

In 1807 the wealthy connoisseur, Thomas Hope, produced a book of furniture designs, *Household Furniture & Interior Decoration*, which illustrated pieces made for his own home. Hope had travelled extensively in the Mediterranean to get accurate details of ancient furniture which he now copied or adapted. There was particular interest in Egyptian furniture and decoration after 1798 when Napoleon invaded Egypt and Nelson destroyed the French fleet at the Battle of the Nile. In general, fashionable furniture followed the classical precedent of straight lines, low height and unbroken surfaces. Much admired were glossy, striped and marbled woods, such as rosewood, zebra wood, amboyna, calamander and mahogany.

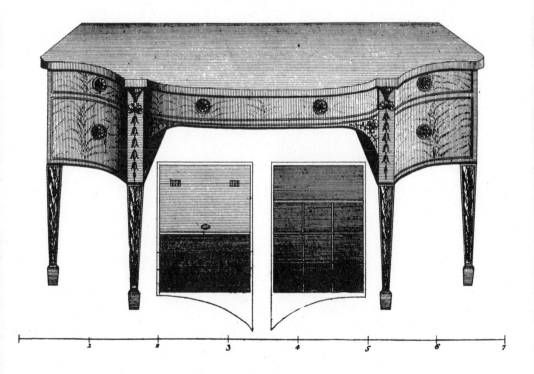

Against this background, a startling effect was obtained by the use of bright brass decoration in the form of lion mask handles and paw feet, trellis work, fretted galleries, colonnettes, bolt heads, studs, honeysuckle, Egyptian sphinx heads and lotus leaves. Classical pieces which were revived included the Greek couch and the *klismos*—the chair with inward curving ('sabre') front legs, broad shoulder board and cane seat, the type soon to become the light 'Trafalgar' chair—circular tables and animal 'monopodia' (lion or chimera heads with a single foot or leg). New Regency pieces included the sofa table and the Carlton House writing table.

This kind of classical furniture required the direction of well-versed designers like Hope to maintain the right standard of accuracy. Unfortunately, the needs of the trade, uncontrolled by the demands of scholarship, led inevitably to degeneration. Sheraton's *Cabinet Dictionary* (1803), which introduced features of the new style, showed in general a firm firm control over design. But *A Collection of Designs for Household Furniture and Interior Decoration*, published in 1808 by a cabinet-maker, George Smith, attempted unsuccessfully to popularize the new taste. He borrowed freely but without real understanding from the fashionable designers of the day and tended to mix styles incongruously.

It is evident that by the end of the Napoleonic Wars (1815) the old classical supremacy was being challenged and overthrown. This was not done hastily. Indeed, many of the trends which are said to have begun after 1830, the year of George IV's death and the one taken by tradition to mark the final dating of genuine antiques, can be discerned well before 1800. The Industrial Revolution was changing the structure of society, making long-accepted notions obsolete and providing craftsmen with many new materials to work with. Since the mid-eighteenth century writers and architects had been interested in the picturesque, a theory which, originating in the landscape paintings of Claude Lorraine, Salvator Rosa and Nicolas Poussin, had encouraged the idea of freedom in design. There was a revival of interest in historic styles. An important aspect of which was played by the association of ideas which saw beauty not necessarily inherent in an object, but was the product of aesthetic ideas which the object aroused. The time was therefore ripe for challenging established attitudes and experimenting with new ones. The Industrial Revolution encouraged experiment and, further, the historical revivals may also be partly explained by a yearning for the past in an age which was changing more rapidly than any other in history.

Above all, there was a new concept of comfort. Leisure and comfort by the 1830s were regarded as the due reward for the hard-working people who were leading the world in industrial output and whose efforts were producing the abundance of goods that could make this comfort possible. More English people than ever before could now have a place of their own and the means to furnish it. Upholstery materials were being produced in the factories more abundantly and more cheaply. Deep-sprung upholstery covered the former elegant outline of seat furniture in this overriding search for comfort, encouraging the decline in the form of furniture which was evident after Victoria's accession in 1837.

But it must not be thought that all Victorian furniture was degenerate. At one time all post-1830 furniture was dismissed as too badly designed to be worth serious study, but recent research has revealed that it contains much of interest. In the application of mechanisation to furniture, in which Sheraton's pioneer work has been referred to, some notable achievements were made. Many patents were taken out for ingeniously contrived gadgets. These made furniture more adaptable, by raising and lowering the seats and backs of chairs, couches and beds and by extending and contracting furniture. Indeed, 'patent' became for a time a fashionable description of all furniture of this kind, whether officially patented or not. Much attention is being paid today to this class of furniture for it represents a close alliance between engineering skill and high-quality cabinet-making. This stressed function and excluded unnecessary ornament, and indeed has many lessons for modern designers of machine-made furniture. Patent furniture was often concerned with pieces made for invalids,

41

and this can be related to the general improvement in medical knowledge and services, and the special needs of the wounded in the long Napoleonic Wars. Such furniture could be easily adapted for domestic use, thus encouraging further the search for comfort. But as inventive genius was gradually tempted into being merely a provider of comfort, ornament

This walnut chair with porcelain plaque of Prince Albert was made by Henry Eyles of Bath and shown at the Great Exhibition, 1851. It has an unusual delicacy for its time.

began to be emphasised at the expense of functionalism. The final blow came with the Great Exhibition of 1851, at the Crystal Palace, London. The temptation had proved too great. Exhibitors of furniture, with the prospects of huge crowds coming to view their products, elaborated them to excess. This was sheer exhibitionism, novelty for novelty's sake, and England's lead in the precise functionalism of patent furniture passed into the hands of the United States.

Meanwhile, between 1830 and 1850 four principal styles affected furniture design. They were fashionable in 1833 when J. C. Loudon named them as "the Grecian or modern style, which is by far the most prevalent; the Gothic or perpendicular style, which imitates the lines and angles of the Tudor Gothic Architecture; the Elizabethan style, which combines the Gothic with the Roman or Italian manner; and the style of the age of Louis XIV, or the florid Italian, which is characterised by curved lines and excess of curvilinear ornaments." 'Grecian' was the term for the last fling of the classical in what has been called the 'sub-classical' style. The Gothic and Elizabethan were fashionable because both were regarded as truly national styles, reflecting the sturdy character of England's ancestors and evoking, by association, stirring or sentimental thoughts about the past. But in fact, in those days of little precise knowledge of art history, complete confusion reigned. The so-called 'Elizabethan' style was based mainly on that of the late Stuart period, with much use of spiral turned supports for seats and tables, and cane seats and tall backs for chairs. This style seems to have been inspired by the romanticism of Sir Walter Scott's novels, and indeed the typical Elizabethan chair of the early Victorian period was sometimes called an 'Abbotsford' chair after Scott's home. Even in the case of the Gothic, where there was much greater knowledge of accurate details, the style simply took the form of adding Gothic trimmings to current frameworks. The Louis XIV style—the Louis Quatorze as it was then called—was the only eighteenth century revival among the historic styles and this can be explained by the resumption of cultural ties with France where

43

the furniture styles of the *ancien régime* had been revived when the Bourbon monarchy was restored in 1815. Here again there was confusion, for in the efforts to introduce their own versions of the Louis Quatorze, English craftsmen decorated the furniture with the gilded scrolls and curves (as Loudon notes) more typical of the rococo of Louis Quinze. As the Louis Quatorze and Louis Quinze were so inextricably mixed, a number of designers preferred to use the simpler comprehensive term of the 'Old French Style'.

The historical revivals were taken up by commercial producers of furniture with little understanding, their object being to cater for the increasing mass of consumers and to pander to their love of ostentation. Much of the decoration was cheap to produce—a good reason, of course, for employing it. The turned members and strapwork ornament of the Elizabethan style were quickly made by machine; so too were carved sections. Furniture mass-produced by machinery was still some time away, but many of the preliminary processes of furniture-making—sawing, planing, moulding, fretwork, mortising and tenoning—were mechanised. Early Victorian furniture demonstrates the pattern current throughout the Queen's reign, the tug-of-war between industry, anxious to produce as much as possible as cheaply as possible, and thoughtful, progressive firms and designers who were alive to falling standards of taste and aimed to maintain or revive furniture of the highest quality.

Contrary to widely accepted notions, early Victorian furniture was mostly well made from very good materials. The standard of craftsmanship remained high, and the Victorian cabinet-maker had an even greater choice of fine timbers than his Georgian predecessor, now that the forests of Africa, Australia and New Zealand were being tapped. Much furniture of the time still has an easy charm. The proliferation of styles continued—Whitaker's *Treasury of Designs* of 1847 adds to Loudon's four styles the Italian, Renaissance, Tudor and François Premier—but we also find attractive light 'fly' drawing room chairs, wicker-back bedroom chairs, 'balloon-back' chairs which established a new shape for dining and drawing rooms, Windsor chairs continuing their long tradition of simple straightforward country pieces, interesting functional furniture of the 'patent' type, and the beginnings of careful efforts to find a style that really responded to the unique condition of the 1850s. There were also many experiments with new materials, not always successful or attractive, but showing a worthy enterprise. One fashionable material which was not new but was revived with a new process of manufacture was papier mâché which was used for small articles and occasionally, on wooden or metal frames, for larger pieces of furniture. The Great Exhibition of 1851 encouraged the showing of as many novel materials as possible, not always with happy results, for ornament was considered as something separate from function, and basically simple shapes were overloaded with decoration. The Exhibition, however, did bring home to discerning designers the appalling decline in standards since the beginning of the century. The standard of the exhibits was fiercely criticised and the next London Exhibition, held in 1862, was sponsored to try to correct the worst follies of 1851.

It is strange that the man now recognised as one of the first great reformers of the nineteenth century designed in the Gothic style. This was A. W. N. Pugin (1812–52), a convert to Roman Catholicism, who in his short but frantically busy life designed many churches for his co-religionists and turned his attention to designing in many crafts. In his furniture Pugin, instead of merely adding Gothic details superficially to existing forms, planned the ornament as an integral part of the design. The construction was openly revealed. No attempt, for instance, was made to hide the pegs which secured mortise and tenon joints. In contrast to his contemporaries, Pugin recognised construction as inherently attractive for its own sake. He thus stressed integrity, for constructional methods were there for all to see. In addition, Pugin advocated that ornament should be based on nature and he designed flat patterns and carved decoration with a charm and vigour all their own.

# Techniques of Furniture-Making

An understanding of the techniques of making and decorating furniture is essential for anyone genuinely interested in antique furniture. It will ensure better appreciation and recognition of the principal styles and can be a safeguard against fakes and copies. With such knowledge one will know what parts of a piece of furniture to examine closely to test its authenticity.

Traditional hand techniques were the rule until the nineteenth century when a certain amount of mechanisation was introduced, but this was almost entirely for the preliminary processes of woodworking and not, as is sometimes assumed, for the complete making of furniture. One exception to hand work was the lathe, operated by the treadle, on which the turner turned pieces of wood into the required shapes by operating his chisel against the timber.

As was noted above, oak ruled the furniture scene for centuries. The tree was felled and the trunk usually quartered; that is, split along its length into four sections. Each quarter was cut towards the centre as this made the timber less inclined to warp and so more durable. Oak cut this way also showed the medullary rays, the characteristic silver grain or figure. Throughout the medieval period and until late Tudor times the log was generally split with beetle and wedge and its surface trimmed with an adze. This was a kind of axe, its cutting edge at right angles to its haft, which was used rather like a pickaxe, the user standing above the timber which was flat on the ground, and allowing the adze to fall and lightly shave the surface. This tool gave early oak furniture its slightly uneven or faceted surface, compared with the perfectly smooth surface produced by a plane. Later, wood was sawn across the top of a saw-pit by two men handling a large, two-handed saw. The task of the bottom sawyer, working in the dark pit and getting the full effect of the shower of sawdust from above, became synonymous with drudgery of the worst kind.

The major constructional developments of medieval furniture sprang from attempts to prevent oak from splitting across the grain. This often occurred when the timber was secured by nails or oak pins. The reason for this is that oak expands and contracts as a result of variable atmospheric conditions. Early chests, for instance, were constructed of six boards nailed or pinned together, and in fact this kind of chest, despite its clumsy appearance, continued to be made until well into the seventeenth century, though by that time thinner boards were used. In the thirteenth century another type of chest employed a front consisting of a single plank fitted into grooves in the wide uprights (or stiles) and secured by pegs. But in each type the wood tended to split, a serious matter when chests were so often used to store valuables. The solution to the problem was the use of the 'panel and frame', a technique which reached England from Flanders in the fifteenth century. A rectangular framework, composed of vertical stiles and horizontal rails, was secured by 'mortise and tenon' joints, the projecting section (tenon) of the rail fitting into the corresponding socket (mortise) of the stile. Oak panels with tapered sides were fitted into grooves on the inside of the frames while these were being assembled, and were thus given a certain freedom of movement which allowed for warping and prevented splitting. This new method of construction amounted to a technological revolution. Panel and frame had to be treated as units of design and their dimensions and proportions had to be carefully worked out beforehand. Much more precision of construction was necessary. The joiner became the principal furniture crafts-man, responsible for everything—chests, chairs, doors and tables, as well as wall panelling—involving the mortise and tenon joint. His kind of furniture—joinery—was altogether lighter, stronger and better proportioned than its predecessor, and its introduction clearly marked the beginning of a new era. The early frames on panelled furniture were assembled

47

without glue and were held by pegs which were roughly squared and tapered oak pins driven hard through holes bored in the mortised member and the corresponding tenon. Once they were tightly wedged the pegs were trimmed off flush with the framing. In time, however, pegs are found standing a little proud of the framing, this being due to the shrinkage of the latter.

The primitive carving on early medieval chests was of the chip or scratch variety, the former, of geometric form, being carried out by removing the pattern from the wood's surface, the latter, an even simpler method, being no more than scoring the surface of the wood with a pointed tool. All this could be done by the carpenter or joiner. For the more sophisticated work—Gothic carving, Biblical scenes and the like found sometimes with remarkable elaboration on later medieval chests—the specialist carver was naturally responsible. In the Elizabethan period sunk carving became fashionable. In this work the pattern was left on the surface of the wood by cutting away the background. This method was employed for strapwork carving or for repeated patterns such as the 'guilloche' (interlaced circles) and 'lunettes' (semicircles), found particularly on the friezes of tables and court cupboards. Sometimes these friezes had a repeated pattern of sunk half-round grooves or channels, and these were gouged out.

One of the oldest methods of decorating furniture was with the turned or 'thrown' work produced by the turner on his lathe. The earliest patterns were very simple spindle shapes, forms of knob- or ball-turning made by small cuts or shallow hollows. The turner socketed the turned sections into the appropriate supports, the 'rungs' of turned spindles, for example, into the uprights of the type of chair now known as a 'ladder-back'. Another type of thrown chair had a flat triangular seat with a strong turned post at each corner, the two front posts being linked by turned arms to a horizontal shoulder board fixed at the back post, while all three posts were united just above floor level with turned stretchers. Many varieties of this kind of chair were made until well into the seventeenth century.

They are the ancestors of the modern Windsor chair.

In the Tudor Period the turner produced the bulbous supports which were so characteristic of the time, and also, under the growing influence of the Renaissance, classic columns with plain shafts and carved capitals. The bulbs on Elizabethan furniture could be built up by gluing four sections to a central square post and then turning them into circular form. For comparatively short lengths, however, such as those on press cupboards, the bulbs could be turned out of the solid. Their carved decoration often took the form of acanthus on the lower leaf and gadrooning on the upper section, a fashionable shape was the 'cup and cover', the domed top resembling the cover of the chalice or cup-shaped body. The more ornate features of this turning disappeared in the early seventeenth century, when diameters were gradually reduced in size. In their place emphasis was laid on spindle and baluster forms and, at about the middle of the century, on knob or on ball and reed. In the otherwise sober decoration of the Cromwellian Period it is surprising to find more than a touch of ornateness in the turned work, for instance, on gate-leg tables. The early seventeenth century also saw the development of a new form of applied ornament, for which the turner was responsible. This was the 'split' baluster; a turned baluster split down the middle to form two matching halves and glued to the surface of the furniture.

The other fashionable Elizabethan decoration, 'inlay', was known at the time as 'markatre'. This must never be confused with the marquetry of the late Stuart Period, for the latter was veneered decoration applied to the surface while inlay was the method of setting woods of contrasting colours below the surface (to about $\frac{1}{8}$ inch) of the wooden ground. Chequered and floral patterns were the most popular, the former found where straight lines were desired, as on the friezes of tables, the latter more appropriately filling complete panels. The chief woods employed for inlay included pear, sycamore, box, holly, ebony and bog oak.

The introduction of veneering from the Continent at the

beginning of the reign of Charles II brought about a change in the construction and decoration of furniture which was as important as the introduction of the panel and frame in the fifteenth century. Professional veneer sawyers, working in pairs, sawed thin sheets of wood from blocks chosen for their attractive figure or colour. These sheets had to be glued to carefully prepared surfaces of the carcase to show off the figure or colour to the best advantage. The traditional panel and frame technique could not provide the necessary surface for the new methods, and though joinery never disappeared from the furniture scene—open frames with mortise and tenon joints were indispensable for chairs, tables and stools, and panels were still structurally necessary for the backs of carcases and for large doors such as those on bookcases—it was now plainly outdated in the fashionable world. The cabinet-maker became established as the chief craftsman in furniture making. The most fashionable wood was walnut, and the most highly-prized varieties came from the Continent, particularly from Grenoble, where the timber was considered to have the best figure of all. As this wood was expensive to import, its use as a veneer sprang from economic as well as aesthetic considerations, though there was bound to be a certain amount of waste in preparing the wood as so much of the beautiful figure was lost in sawdust. Saw-cut veneers were thick by modern standards, varying from about $\frac{1}{8}$ to $\frac{1}{16}$ inch, compared with the paper thinness of present day knife and rotary cut commercial veneers.

Successive veneers sawn from the same block of wood repeated its figure, allowing the cabinet-maker to make full use of the decorative effects of matching, reversing or opposing the patterns on suitable grounds, such as the drawer fronts of bureaux, tallboys and chests of drawers, or the tops of tables. 'Quartering' was the method of laying four veneers with the figure twice reversed. Oak was an unsuitable base for veneering because of its tendency to move in the atmosphere which unsettled the veneers. Much more stable and suitable was imported deal which had the additional merit of being cheap. Particularly interesting and attractive figures for veneers were the 'crotches', taken from the junction of branch and trunk, 'oyster-pieces', cut from the branches of small trees, and 'burrs', the abnormal growths on tree trunks or roots that provided intricate, irregular patterns. Depending on the nature of the wood the latter were usually thicker than other veneers and more difficult to apply as they tended to curl. In addition to walnut the most prized woods included elm, ash, mulberry, yew, maple and kingwood. Laburnum and olive produced the best oyster-pieces.

Attractive as veneers were, their decorative effect was further increased in several ways. On larger surfaces the veneers were laid in cross-banded borders composed of short strips of veneer with the grain running across the width; another narrow inner border had 'herring-bone' banding, so called from the slanting small strips of veneer of two contrasting colours. This herring-bone border often replaced cross-banding on smaller surfaces such as drawer fronts. A constructional change was made necessary by the use of veneers. The old through or common dovetail had one defect in that the end grain of the sides showed through the drawer front and made an unsatisfactory ground for the veneer. The remedy was the 'lapped' or 'stopped' dovetail which did not go through the drawer front and showed the end grain only at the sides.

One of the most brilliantly successful decorative techniques which will always be associated with the late Stuart Period is that of 'marquetry'. Here the effect was obtained by employing as many different coloured veneers as possible, with occasionally other materials, such as ivory and mother-of-pearl, to build up floral and foliate compositions. Where a geometrical pattern was desired, a variation of marquetry, known as 'parquetry', was employed, based on oyster-pieces. Considerable trouble was taken to get veneers of the right shade of colour and, if necessary, woods were dyed, stained, bleached or scorched in hot sand. Sycamore, stained greenish-grey and used for leaves in floral marquetry, acquired the name of 'harewood' (it was also known as silverwood in the eighteenth century). The marquetry cutter, a very skilled craftsman, set to work by first drawing the design on paper then pricking through on further sheets if he wanted duplicates. The pattern was pasted on top of sheets of veneer which were fastened by panel pins or by interleaved sheets of glued paper. The lines of the drawing were then worked through by the craftsman with a fine frame saw. Pieces of each layer were carefully chosen and arranged on the ground to make the required pattern which was held together by a sheet of glued paper then fastened on to the carcase. An idea of the immense skill as well as the labour that were needed for this craft can be obtained by inspecting a cabinet on which the doors, inside and out, the fronts of the interior drawers and the frieze of the supporting stand have all been covered with marquetry, still a blaze of colour and still, with its multitude of veneers, in excellent condition.

About 1690 a distinct change in the style of marquetry became apparent. The bright floral designs which had been fashionable since 1660 began to give way to quieter colours, except on long-case clocks which persisted with floral marquetry. Intricate arabesques were now the mode, and for these only two shades of colour were used, a dark one, such as walnut, for the ground, and a light one, holly, box, pear or sycamore, for the pattern. This change represented the English version of the intricate marquetry in tortoiseshell, metal and wood which André-Charles Boulle (1642–1732) and other craftsmen were producing at that time in France. The version of arabesque marquetry which has been given the modern name of 'seaweed' marquetry because of its involved patterns seems to have been a peculiarly English innovation. Early in the eighteenth century the fashion for marquetry died out. There was a return to plainer veneers and, with the gradual introduction of mahogany, to carving.

It is perhaps difficult today to imagine the extraordinary effect which the import of oriental lacquer had upon European countries in the seventeenth century. In no other European country did it play so important a part in furniture as it did in England. True lacquer came from China and Japan, and its source was the resin from the tree *Rhus vernicifera*. This resin was coloured with pigment and then painted in many coats over a thin wooden foundation. The brilliant and durable finish which lacquer gave was the result of centuries-old practice. Two main kinds of surface decoration were found on specimens imported into Europe, one with the ornament in relief and the other with incised designs cut in the surface and then coloured. The latter type was known as 'Bantam' work. Imported lacquer naturally stimulated Europeans to search for imitations, but their substitutes failed to match either the brilliance or the durability of the original. The English imitation—japan—employed varnish and paint colours and was coated over a base of whiting and size to form the ground. The design was painted on in gilding and colours mixed with gum-arabic. A paste of gum-arabic and whiting, also coloured and gilded, was added to give details in relief. Bantam work could be imitated by cutting out the appropriate design from the ground of whiting and size, and then colouring and gilding it. The great age of English japanning occurred in the early eighteenth century when imported lacquer was practically excluded from the home market by high tariffs. Much of the japanned furniture of this time, however, was discarded when the decoration lost its colour or flaked and chipped. Some surviving examples show the prevailing fondness for bright colours such as reds, greens, yellows and blues, but a close inspection of lacquered and japanned furniture will soon prove the extraordinary vitality of the former.

Gilded furniture has a long history behind it, but it became particularly fashionable after the Restoration and in the first quarter of the eighteenth century. The gold leaf was applied to furniture in two distinct ways, water gilding or oil gilding. In each case the ground was 'gesso', the composition of whiting (chalk) and parchment size already referred to as the base for japanned work. This was applied in many coats to the wood to procure a smooth, hard and even surface. In water gilding a special clay was brushed on to the gesso and thoroughly soaked with water, and the gold leaf was then applied speedily as the water dried out quickly. This method produced burnished and matt finishes. A second application of gold was sometimes made for brightly burnished work. Oil gilding was a slower, less skilled and cheaper process which was also more durable than water gilding. It could not, however, be burnished.

The evolution of the chest of drawers from the mule chest to a rudimentary modern form by about 1650 has already been noted. In the sixteenth and early seventeenth centuries the side of the drawer, usually of stout oak, was nailed to the rebated front (with a rectangular recess on its edge) and had a groove which enabled the drawer to slide on a runner (or bearer) fixed to the inside of the carcase. In the early seventeenth century the first crude dovetails began to appear. They were wide and had coarse pins (the members of the joint into which the dovetails fit), the end grain being exposed on the two surfaces ('through' dovetailing). After 1660 there were two notable advances in construction. Firstly, the groove and runner method went out of fashion, except in country areas where traditional techniques lingered on, and the drawers now moved on runners which formed part of the horizontal division between them. Secondly, the dovetails became smaller and thus increased in number. Sometimes the backs of drawers were also dovetailed to the sides and the latter might have their top edges rounded. Another improvement was the introduction of the 'lapped' (stopped) dovetail which prevented the end grain from showing at the front and thus provided a much securer ground for the veneer.

The development of mouldings on furniture is always worth study. These are the decorative pieces of wood which usually project from the surfaces of various parts of furniture such as the frames surrounding panels, the edges of tables, cornices, friezes and plinths. They can also be incised, as in the example of those struck on the stiles and rails of panelled framing. Both kinds were found on early framed furniture, on chests, for instance. A 'scratched' moulding was struck along the edges of the framing round the panel, usually on the bottom edge of the top rail and on the inside edge of the corner posts. These mouldings were not carried all along the edge but stopped short of the corners where stile and rail met. Mouldings were also worked in the solid, particularly on the edges of the intermediate stiles. 'Mitres,' the diagonal joints formed by two mouldings when they meet at right angles, were laboriously chiselled in stonemasons' fashion, hence their name 'mason's' mitre. This process was discontinued in the sixteenth century when the true or joiner's mitre came into use, the mitre being worked on the actual joint.

In the first half of the seventeenth century it was fashionable to decorate furniture with applied mouldings which were glued into position. These may be found in addition to mouldings in the solid. The picturesqueness of the results is well illustrated in the early chests of drawers, of about 1650, which had elaborate geometric mouldings applied to projecting panels of hexagonal or octagonal forms; further ornament came from inlay of bone, ivory and mother-of-pearl and various woods. These ornamental mouldings and inlays seem to have been inspired by earlier Flemish and German models. Another form of applied decoration has already been described—the split baluster which decorated cupboards, chairs, chests, chests of drawers and headboards of beds.

With the advent of the walnut period, the mouldings used by cabinet-makers were nearly all based on examples found in classical architecture. They were shaped to the required profile by the moulding plane or scratch stock and were covered with cross-grain veneer; that is, with the grain running across the width. Taller pieces of the late Stuart Period, such as tallboys and chests on stands, had bold cornices made by the addition of mouldings to form a 'cavetto' (concave) or 'swell' (convex) frieze. The swell or 'pulvenated' frieze was a particular feature of the Queen Anne Period.

Much attention was paid at the time to the smaller mouldings round drawer fronts, and the changes in their shape and position on the furniture form a reliable guide to dating. These walnut mouldings were cross-banded, strips of veneer cut across the grain being glued to a groundwork of deal or oak with the grain running lengthwise. From about 1660 until the beginning of Anne's reign half round mouldings or beadings were applied to the rails of the carcase between the drawers. By 1695 double half round or reeded mouldings, or sometimes three together, were also to be found. Early in Anne's reign a distinct change occurred in that the mouldings were no longer applied to the rails but to the edge of the drawer itself, leaving the rails plain. At first an 'ovolo lip' moulding, projecting from the edge of the rebated drawer front, came into fashion. This overlapped the rails and had the advantage both of concealing the gap between rail and drawer and making the latter more dust-proof. Then, from about 1730, as mahogany gradually came into wider use, 'cock' beading, a half round bead fixed to the extreme edge of the drawer, was adopted. Mahogany drawer fronts were made in the solid and the cock beading, also in the solid, was worked into the rebated edges. This beading became the established drawer edging for the rest of the eighteenth century. Little change was made in drawer construction except that after about 1740 the general tendency was to use timber for the bottom of the drawer in which the grain ran from side to side and not, as was the practice previously, from back to front. Although this change in direction of the grain is a good pointer to age it is not an infallible one as exceptions to the generally accepted practice are to be found from time to time.

An informative contemporary publication, Moxon's *Mechanick Exercises*, which was issued in parts between 1677 and 1683, throws much light on the tools and constructional methods of the late Stuart era. It has a section devoted to turning and shows that the twist or spiral turning which was so characteristic of Charles II's reign—it was used on the legs and stretchers of tables, chairs and stands and on the back uprights of chairs—was executed by a special contrivance fitted on the lathe ("you set it to that slope you intend the swash on your work shall have."). This was necessary as the lathe normally only permitted cuts at right angles to the axis, and not at an angle of inclination denoted by 'swash'. Double twists were worked with two spirals and finished by hand on the inner side, this kind of work being sometimes known as double rope or 'barley sugar' twist. For double open twist, consisting of two open spirals, the wood was first bored through its entire length, the double spiral was then completed on the lathe and the hollows were gouged through to the central hole. This was a strikingly decorative method of turning but the resulting member was obviously not strong enough for chair legs.

As chair-making became a separate and specialised craft in the seventeenth century standard terms began to be applied to the different parts of the chair. With the advent of the curvilinear chair at the close of the century the back uprights, which were continuations of the back legs, were curved in serpentine form, becoming concave towards the top at the level of the sitter's shoulders. The top or 'yoke' rail, or cresting, was fitted into the uprights. The central wide splat, often of vase or urn shape, was framed to the top rail and into the shoe-piece, the special projection fixed to the top of the back seat rail to form a secure base for the splat. The frame of the seat consisted of four separate rails tenoned into the legs. Angle blocks or brackets were screwed into the corners of the rails to give additional strength and to support the drop-in seat.

The cabriole leg which came into fashion with the curvilinear chair did not acquire its name until Victorian times. 'Cabriole' in the late Georgian Period denoted an upholstered armchair and a French easy chair. The term was derived from the Italian *capriola*, a goat's leap, and was used in France to describe a leap in dancing. Not surprisingly, the earliest version of the leg abroad was an animal's leg ending in a hoof foot. Great skill was involved in its making. First of all, suitable blocks of walnut or, later, mahogany, about three inches square and eighteen inches long, were carefully selected. The whole leg, except the shoulder pieces, had to be made from each block. Outline curves were marked on two adjacent sides from a thin wooden or card template. The upper part of the leg, above the knee, was left as a block to be mortised for the tenons of two seat rails. The next stage was to cut the curves on the wood with a large bow-saw. Some cabriole legs were left as curved legs of rectangular section, but usually the block was placed in the lathe and the pad foot was turned (this of course was not done if the foot was to be carved), and then, with the block once more in the vice, the leg was rounded and shaped with the spokeshave and rasp. It became customary to dowel or glue a suitably shaped shoulder piece to each side of the knee, thus giving it a broader appearance.

The first cabriole legs on English chairs were narrow and had hoof feet joined by stretchers. The latter were discarded when the knee pieces were widened. The hoof foot was at the same time replaced by the pad or club. About 1710 some cabriole legs had a carved honeysuckle or shell on the knee, but most were left plain. The most famous of the terminals to the cabriole leg, the 'claw-and-ball' foot, also came into fashion about 1710 and was to enjoy a vogue of some fifty years. The great age of the carved cabriole came in the second quarter of the century when the remarkable qualities of mahogany became evident. This was the so-called 'lion period', but in addition to the lion's head, paws and mane there were other fashionable carved motifs, including acanthus, eagle's feathers and female and Indian masks. The tapered or cylindrical leg, influenced by French models, was found in the neo-classical period and represents the last phase of the cabriole (it was to be revived frequently in the next century). Exceptionally fine chairs had all four legs of cabriole form but normally only the front pair were so shaped. Real appreciation of the meticulous care taken by craftsmen in matching the cabriole legs on their chairs can only be obtained by a close examination of good examples.

Metal mounts on furniture, principally hinges, locks and handles, are an important guide to dating and authenticity. Nearly all the types of hinges found on eighteenth-century furniture can be traced back to prototypes in the late medieval period. Early chests and aumbries used much scrolled ironwork to provide protection as well as ornament. The 'strap' hinge, in use on heavy doors and lids, had a long plate, either plain or decorated, fastened on the surface of the furniture. Later the 'butterfly' hinge, resembling the shape of the butterfly's wings, came into use. This was the prototype of the 'cocks-head' hinge which was found on the doors of seventeenth-century cupboards.

After 1600 metalwork on furniture became generally much lighter in character with the appearance of joined pieces. The considerable increase in the production of furniture also gave more scope to the metalworker. Metal fittings now became the responsibility of the locksmith who made all the mounts as well as locks, and worked with great skill in cold metal, replacing the blacksmith whose medium had been red-hot iron. Locksmithing produced more delicate and precise work. A conspicuous feature of the Stuart Period was the 'chamfering' (bevelling) of the edges of mounts.

Until about 1650 nails, and not screws, were used to secure locks and hinges. These hand-made nails are easily recognizable by their faceted and slightly arched heads. When screws came into use in the early walnut period their threads were filed by hand and they did not taper to a sharp point. Lathe-turned screws came in after 1750. Modern machine-made screws with gimlet-pointed heads date from the time of the Great Exhibition of 1851.

The cocks-head hinge had a counterpart in the 'H' hinge, each taking its (modern) name from the shape of its outline and each found on the surface. The former, curving outwards, had thinner metal at its extremities while the latter had two vertical plates of uniform thickness.

While iron continued in use on country pieces, the Post-Restoration Period saw the introduction of brass as the almost exclusive metal on cabinet furniture. Brass had many virtues—a good colour and polish and a softness which made for easy working and precise finishing; moreover, it could be cast into repeated and accurate patterns. Birmingham now became the great centre of brass casting. Its brass-founders issued pattern books of furniture mounts which set the fashion in England and had a large following in America.

Brass was used for the lavishly ornamental mounts, copied

59

from the Chinese, with which cabinet-makers decorated japanned cabinets after 1660. These consisted of large double-lock plates and broad corner plates. Brass handles followed well defined fashion changes. In the later Stuart Period the 'tear-drop' or 'acorn' handle, taking its name from the bulbous drop attached to a circular back-plate, was in wide use. Early versions of this type had been heavy in form and occasional florid examples in silver appeared on chests of drawers and cabinets. Another type had a fan-tail drop attached to a star-shaped plate. The back-plates had a split metal tang which went through the drawer front and opened out at the back for fastening.

In the early eighteenth century handles took on an entirely new form, that of a loop attached to an ornamental chamfered back-plate. The ends of the loop were attached to cast knobs and the latter were secured to the drawer by a pin on which a nut was threaded on the inside. The back-plates were at first solid, sometimes decorated with punch marks and engraved lines, but later (c. 1710–30) their centres were removed to form scrolled outlines. The escutcheon (keyhole) commonly took the form of a cartouche with surface orna-ment. It was later pierced to conform with the decoration of the back-plates, but about 1750 it was often of very simple shape, even with ornate handles, no more than a small flush brass plate.

About 1750 the loop handle was attached to two small circular plates (or 'roses'). At the same time furniture in the new rococo style often had flamboyantly scrolled handles. Their quality was not high, illustrating the difficulty en-countered by English craftsmen attempting the chasing (carving in metal) in the French manner. Indeed, the best mounts in this taste were almost certainly imported from France or made in England by French craftsmen. But Birmingham became the centre of English manufacture of 'ormolu' after Matthew Boulton established his Soho Works there in 1762. This material, which previously had to be imported from France, was produced by coating chased brass (or bronze) with an amalgam of mercury and gold dust and then firing the metal to a high temperature. This caused the mercury to evaporate leaving the gold fast adhered to the metal which could be brightly burnished. In the Adam Period ormolu was used as running frets, terminals (often ram's heads), festoons of husks and similar classical ornament on furniture of the best quality.

In simpler furniture of the neo-classic period the same kind of classical ornament appeared on the continuous brass back-plates which were now revived. Their form was novel—sheet brass which was ornamented by mechanical stamping in a process patented in 1779 by John Marston and Edward Bellamy, two Birmingham brass-founders. The stamped back-plates were usually of circular or oval form, the handle taking the same shape and hanging from the top of the plate. There are, however, examples of loop handles attached to stamped roses. Two types of handle on Regency furniture are very characteristic of the period, a small brass knob, and a cast lion's mask with a ring in its mouth. During the early Victorian Period knobs of the same wood as the furniture came into fashion as a substitute for brass. Loudon's *Encyclopaedia* in 1833 describes these knobs as "comparatively new" and explains that "they harmonise better and do not tarnish."

Table construction is another useful guide to dating. The method of extending a table top to double its length which came into use about 1550 is still found today. The two draw-leaves were placed one at each side of a small plank fixed across the under-frame of the table, under the main table top. Each leaf pulled out on two runners working in slots in the table frame, these runners being sloped at an angle which allowed each leaf, when fully extended, to rest level with the main table top. To prevent the draw-leaves from coming out too far, the runners were fitted with small blocks or stops which rested hard against the table frame when the leaves were extended to their correct length.

When the draw-leaf table went out of fashion, gate-leg tables were used for meals. Some of these were large and required two gates at each side to support the flaps. The general type had four legs at each side, two forming the gate which had stretchers at the top and bottom. 'Halvings' (cross joints with half the timber in each member cut away to provide flush surfaces) were cut in the stretchers of the table and in the base of the gate-leg to enable the gate to shut close. Various kinds of joints were used between the flap and table top but the 'rule' joint became the established type in the Georgian Period. This device was so shaped that it prevented a gap showing when the leaf was lowered.

Several types of gate-leg tables can be found, large and small, with semicircular or rectangular flaps. Seventeenth-century examples had trestle ends, then trestle feet with turned baluster supports. Dining tables could be built up of two semicircular units joined together for the meal, with sometimes a rectangular table, also gate-legged, in the centre. All these tables, when not required for a meal, could form side tables, with their gates shut. One often finds these components sold now as separate side tables. An attractive form of gate-leg table made after 1765 had extremely slender turned supports and was given the very appropriate con-temporary name of 'spider leg' table.

When the cabriole leg was introduced, the table with a hinged circular or rectangular top became very fashionable. The hinged half folded back on the fixed half and thus formed a side table when not in use. When the hinged section was unfolded it was supported on one or two of the cabriole legs (depending on the size of the flap) which swung out on wooden hinges fixed to the frame. The elegant card tables of the early eighteenth century worked on this principle, using one hinged cabriole leg to support the opened top. The corners were rounded and dished (slightly sunk in the surface) to hold candlesticks, and oval wells were made in the top for the coins or counters. It seemed that the open table, with one leg swung out, appeared ungainly, and from about 1705 to 1765 many card tables were made with a folding frame which opened out in concertina fashion by extending two legs.

The two-flap gate-leg table had been a useful piece and its principle was revived after 1765 in the convenient and delightful 'Pembroke' table. The flaps, on metal hinges and closing to a rule joint, were supported on wooden brackets (usually beech) which swung outwards on wooden hinges. Pembroke tables often had a drawer at one end, and a dummy drawer front at the other.

Tripod stands and tables (or 'pillar and claws') were in use throughout the Georgian era and were particularly fashionable from about the middle of the century as tea tables. The tripod foot was made up of three legs of cabriole form dovetailed into the base of the column which was a turned shaft or baluster. A small box-like gallery was hinged to two bearers under the table top. A circular hole in the base of this gallery enabled it to be fitted over the tapered top of the column and be secured by driving in a wedge. If the latter were removed the top could easily be lifted off the column. As the gallery was hinged to the bearers, the top could be swung to a vertical position to stand against the wall when not in use. When the top was swung back again it was securely fastened by a spring catch.

Varieties of small portable tables were popular in late Stuart households. This side table, probably made about the end of Charles II's reign, shows the prevalent fashion for spirally turned legs, flat waved stretchers and marquetry.

# The Care and Renovation of Furniture

Antique furniture can be used in almost every case as its original owners intended. With careful attention it can—and should—be kept in first-class condition, thus improving both its appearance and value. Every collector is proud of his pieces and anxious to show them at their best. To keep furniture in the best possible condition two main lines of procedure should be followed. The first is to protect furniture from its potential enemies—damp, wood-boring insects, sunlight and heat. Damp may not merely arise from the state of a room or wall; a fine table top can easily be ruined by standing a leaky bowl of water on it. Strong sunlight can cause wood to fade badly so that the position of finely veneered piece of furniture relative to a large window is clearly a matter for concern. Heat from an open fire or radiator can cause serious damage as has been proved in recent years by the deterioration of old furniture in centrally-heated rooms. The problems of central heating and that of woodworm and its remedies are discussed in more detail below.

The second line of policy to follow is always to put repairs and restoration into the hands of competent and experienced craftsmen. There are certain specialist fields such as veneering, marquetry, gilding and turning where tampering by an amateur can have only disastrous results. Even apparently simple operations, such as re-gluing a joint, renewing beading or replacing a strip of veneer, are often more complicated than appear at first sight. Sometimes, for example, an attempt will be made to repair a joint without the realisation that a single defective joint can well have strained the whole structure of a carcase and requires professional treatment. The repair of clock mechanism is another matter which only a clockmaker experienced in old time-pieces can deal with efficiently, and tinkering by an owner who has no detailed knowledge may cause considerable harm.

Fine polished woods have a subtle patina which is one of the most appealing features of antique furniture, whether the piece be of solid wood or veneered. Attractive variety of grain and rich warm tones are the results of generations of careful treatment and the preservation of a good patina is of the first importance. An effective polish should protect the surface of the wood, bring out all its attractive features and, at the same time, avoid showing unsightly finger marks. There are many commercial polishes on the market in the form of solids, creams, liquids and sprays. As their quality varies it is advisable to ask a dealer to recommend the one which he himself uses. Many dealers and collectors, however, prefer to use their own polish and what better than that used by the Georgian cabinet-makers themselves. The basic ingredients are described by Sheraton in his *Cabinet Dictionary* of 1803 thus:

"Take bees wax and a small quantity of turpentine in a clear earthen pan and set it over a small fire till the wax unites with the turpentine which it will do by constant stirring about."

Beeswax polish can easily be made at home by shredding the wax and covering the flakes with genuine (not substitute) turpentine, a good blend being three parts of white beeswax to eight parts of turpentine. The wax is dissolved by very vigorous stirring; if the mixture is left overnight the polish is ready for use next morning. Or, as Sheraton suggests, the dissolving process, which is inevitably slow, can be accelerated if the mixture is first gently heated in an old saucepan. The consistency can be gauged by adding wax or turpentine until the polish sets, when it should be like soft butter. If it is too thin the liquid polish may cause harm by flowing into cracks, mounts or locks; if it is too thick it will smear the surface and gradually obscure the tones of the wood. The polish must be kept in a covered container otherwise the wax will harden if left standing. Stirring or gentle heating will restore it to the right consistency when it is required again. A good method of application is by brush, covering about a square foot at a time. Two cloths are useful, one for getting rid of dirt or stain—

this is the function of the turpentine and the amount of dirt left on the cloth will indicate the state of the surface—the other for polishing. Time and patience can work wonders. Excellent results can be obtained on old surfaces by weeks or months of careful and regular application. It is worth remembering that the effectiveness of this polish is very much a matter of the amount of hard work put into the final polishing.

The surface of an old piece of furniture which has been neglected may be covered with years of grime which will need removal before polishing. Another safe home-made cleanser is a mixture, in a bottle, of one part each of turpentine, linseed oil and vinegar with a quarter of a part of methylated spirit. The mixture should be well shaken before use and applied sparingly with cotton wool.

Much antique furniture has been French polished with ingredients made up of shellac dissolved in spirits. French polish came to England from France and quickly caught on after 1815, establishing itself as a popular method of treating furniture throughout the Victorian Period. According to G. A. Siddons's *Cabinet-Maker's Guide* (1830) its purpose was to give "a harder face which shall not be so liable to scratch the varnish and yet have an equally fine face." Good French polish gives a glossy surface, enhances the figure of the wood and can last for some fifty years. Unfortunately inferior brands were made in England and many pieces of old walnut and mahogany furniture were stripped and polished. Also, by about 1850, it became fashionable to stain wood before application. The result was the loss of the incomparable patina of much old furniture. The process was seen and strongly criticised by C. L. Eastlake in his *Hints on Household Taste* (1868): "the present system of French polishing or literally varnishing furniture is destructive of all artistic effect in its appearance because the surface of the wood thus lacquered can never change its colour, or acquire that rich hue which is one of the chief charms of old cabinet-work." Moreover, though it must be admitted that skilled French polishers could produce a splendid surface, it has the disadvantage of being easily marked by drinks, as it is soluble in alcohol, turns white if left in contact with water for any length of time and becomes soft at a fairly low temperature and so can be marked by hot dishes. The effect on table tops can be thus imagined!

Another method of treating surfaces was with varnish, a transparent gum giving a highly glazed effect. Varnish is much less affected than French polish by water or alcohol, but it cracks in time into tiny lines which become filled with dirt and grease, leaving a matted rough surface that obscures the figure and grain. There are several commercial products for removing varnished or French polished surfaces preparatory to using beeswax polish. Even if the piece is of no great value and the surface small, removal should be done with care, using first the stripper applied with cotton wool, then cleaning off with cotton wool soaked in turpentine. If the furniture is valuable, or has been lacquered, or is decorated with inlay, the stripping is best left to the professional.

To the collector whose furniture is otherwise in excellent condition the most pressing problem today is probably that of central heating. The comfortable convenience of this modern amenity has often confronted the dismayed owner with split or distorted large surfaces, panels starting from their frames, joints strained as the old glue is loosened, and veneered and marquetry decoration spoilt. The problem is not solved by having the furniture repaired, often at considerable expense, and then re-submitting it to the same conditions. What happens is that central heating reduces the moisture content of the air of the room and thus of the wood, causing severe shrinkage. It is possible to install humidifiers to control the humidity of a room, but these are expensive items. They are worth while for furniture of particular rarity and high value, and can be placed in a single room where the furniture is kept. Apart from this there are other useful points to bear in mind. Furniture should never be placed near radiators. A valuable piece should be kept in the coolest part of the room where the temperature is maintained at a moderate level, enough for comfort but not too high. Whenever possible, air circulation should be maintained by keeping doors open that do not have to be shut. Some collectors have found it useful to keep bowls of water in the rooms.

Woodworm is a destructive enemy of furniture as its early stages of attack are not easy to detect or combat. The common furniture beetle lays its eggs in the cracks of furniture and the first holes to appear are caused by larvae that bore their way through the wood to the surface and emerge as beetles. To treat any new holes that have appeared is often like locking the stable door after the horse has gone, for the beetles fly off to begin the cycle of mating and egg-laying all over again. As this egg-laying is most likely to occur in the same piece of furniture from which the female emerged, action can profit-ably be taken. Spring is the period when the change from the larval state takes place and this is the time to treat the wood with a worm-killing fluid, of which there are a number on the market. The fluid should be applied under and inside the furniture (it does not normally harm polish) and another application is advisable about September. The process should be repeated regularly for three years, and if the first new holes are sealed with wax, any fresh ones can be detected at once. In badly infested furniture, the holes should be injected with fluid so that it can penetrate the channels left by insects in the wood. Naturally, if the furniture is very badly affected, or if the woodworm is persistent and can be traced to other timber in the house, it is best to call in expert advice.

When a piece of furniture has been exposed to strong sunlight polished surfaces are likely to deteriorate and the underlying wood may bleach. Attempts to restore colour by staining the bleached part are most unwise. This is another matter which certainly requires professional attention. So too is the repair of dents and burns. Dents and bruises in furniture are sometimes tackled by the old remedy of using a damp cloth and hot iron over the affected part. This method has the result of swelling the wood and raising the injured area, but it also penetrates polish and destroys the finish of the wood, and needs a craftsman's skill for complete restoration. However, too much attention need not be paid to getting every scratch, mark or dent out of old furniture. They are the honourable scars of many years of useful work and as long as they are not unsightly they may well provide a more attractive surface than one which has been entirely renewed.

*The Cabinet Maker.*

# Fakes, Forgeries and Copies

This chapter is intended to put the reader on his guard when examining antique furniture, particularly if he intends to purchase. It must first of all be remembered that most pieces of antique furniture have undergone some alteration at one time or another. This is nearly always the result of repairs which were made necessary by a long period—sometimes centuries—of active use. Indeed, such repairs are to be welcomed as a guarantee of age; one should be suspicious from the start of any piece which appears to be in mint condition. Chair and table legs, for instance, which have been broken, and their stretchers snapped off or badly worn down, veneers which have curled up or dropped off, and sections of carved wood and gesso fractured—all these must be replaced to restore the pieces to something like their original serviceable state. It has been computed that the upholstery on well-used seating furniture has been renewed about every thirty years or so as it becomes worn out, and the present covering may be pieces of old upholstery in good condition which have been transferred to the seats, or, more likely, modern materials which sometimes attempt to repeat the pattern and colour of the original upholstery. Surviving seats which have retained their original covers are very rare and naturally command high prices.

Alterations can be the result of changes in fashion as well as of necessary repairs. Drawer handles, for example, have been changed as new shapes or materials have appealed to the owner. These fashion changes, like repairs, are not difficult to detect and their object was to keep the furniture in as good a condition as possible, without any intention to deceive. In a quite different category is the practice of assembling genuine old materials—timber, carvings, inlays, panels, upholstery, gilding and metal fitments—into totally new pieces of furniture. This practice has a long history behind it and was done quite openly before Victoria's reign in order to provide suitable furniture for the current Gothic, Tudor and Elizabethan revivals. In 1833 J. L. Loudon wrote in his *Encyclopaedia of Cottage, Farm and Villa Architecture and Furniture*:

> "We now have upholsterers in London who collect, both in foreign countries and in England, whatever they can find of curious and ancient furniture, including fragments of fittings-up of rooms, altars and religious houses; and rearrange these curious specimens, and adapt them to modern uses."

Sometimes the adaptations of this 'Wardour Street Gothic', as it is now called after the area of London where the practice was particularly rife, are so ludicrous that the deception can be seen at once, as in the examples of late seventeenth clock movements which are found in cases decorated with genuine carved fragments of Jacobean or even earlier origin. As Loudon indicates, many old fragments came from abroad. A large quantity came on the market after the destruction of monastic property in Flanders and elsewhere during the French Revolution. Fine old Flemish panels and carvings turn up in the strangest places.

While anachronisms should be obvious to the student of furniture, the case is quite different with more carefully assembled pieces. The difficulty here is that although the original makers were quite open in what they were doing, and even well-known architects were not above the practice when fitting out their 'period' rooms, in the process of time changes of ownership and a dearth of information about the furniture have inevitably caused confusion, and many fabricated pieces have been passed off as genuine, sometimes by dealers who have not been too scrupulous in enquiring about origins or in revealing the truth—even if it is known to them. Here detection can be a formidable task as all the components are genuinely old.

Difficulty of identification also arises when modern copies of old furniture are made to replace articles destroyed or damaged beyond repair, or to provide a replica of a piece that is the sole survivor of a former pair. Thus one comes across pairs of candles stands, wall lights, side tables and urn stands where the copy exists side by side with the original, and at first glance it is impossible to separate them.

Another source of copied furniture was the Art Furniture Movement of the 1860s and 1870s when reproductions of furniture in the historic styles were done with great skill and care. Such reproductions were not intended to deceive, and reputable makers clearly labelled their furniture. One of the best known firms of this kind, Edwards and Roberts of Wardour Street, London, turned out excellent reproductions of furniture which ranged in style from the sixteenth century onwards. They employed craftsmen whose skill matched that of their Georgian forerunners. After a century of use these reproductions have now acquired the patina of genuine old furniture, and if the tell-tale label is missing it is sometimes impossible even for the expert to be certain of the age. Similarly, in the Arts and Crafts Movement which began in the 1880s a great deal of very skilled reproduction furniture was produced, though in this case the craftsmen showed more individuality in their work.

The main problem is, of course, the faker who deliberately sets out from the beginning to deceive and who, because his trade has been so lucrative, has brought to it both ingenuity and craftsmanship of the highest quality. Like the makers of Loudon's day, the modern faker can use authentic old materials of every kind and can add to them new ones skillfully treated to appear old. New wood, for example, can be given suitable dents, markings, scratches and discoloration to show evidence of long wear. Old gilding can be carefully removed from its original background and applied to such articles as picture frames which are made up partly of old carvings and partly of new. A set of eleven antique chairs can be made up to a dozen by taking one section from each of the eleven originals (e.g. right front leg, left front leg, stretcher, seat rail, etc.), replacing each section with a careful copy, and making these sections, with a modern addition, into number twelve. As each chair is now some eleven-twelfths genuine, deception is comparatively easy.

How, then, can the prospective buyer be certain that he is getting the genuine article? A suspicious frame of mind supported by a sound working knowledge of furniture styles, materials and techniques, is an obvious recommendation, and so, too, is a reputable dealer. The collector must look at as much furniture as he can in shops, museums and private collections, for only in this way can he get the feel of the texture, colour and patina of old wood. Books, photographs and drawings will also give him the necessary information about types of furniture, stylistic changes, structural methods and decorative techniques to put him on his guard if a piece of furniture strikes him as being strange, unusual or clearly inaccurate.

Antique shops contain many 'converted' pieces, consisting of genuine fragments or sections from one piece of furniture 'married' to parts of another—pole screens converted into kettle stands, chests of drawers superimposed on different stands after the original ones have collapsed, circular pillar and claw tables made up by adding the top of one to the upright of another and so forth. It is also possible that a piece has been altered to suit the whim of a previous owner, such as a tall piece cut down to fit into a smaller room. Thus the feet may have been cut off or drastically altered, or a drawer section may have been removed. A craze in the Victorian Period, amounting to vandalism, was to reduce the size of long-case clocks to conform to the prevailing fashion for three-quarter length clocks. In all these cases a good eye for proportions is useful. Fashion changes, again, may lead to paint being cleaned off furniture or, conversely, to the painting over of original decoration.

Drawers should always be examined with a critical eye. It has already been noted that dovetails have a very definite chronological sequence so that it is comparatively easy to see whether they match the age of the drawer. Dovetails became finer as the eighteenth century progressed for the fineness of 'pins' was proof of the craftsman's skill. Modern machine-

73

made dovetails are always regular as pins and tails are a uniform size. It is always worth while to remove drawers for investigation. Their interiors which housed clothes, papers, etc. should have darker wood than the underneath and exterior sides. Where the drawer moves on runners it should show signs of wear underneath, with grooves or channels to correspond to the position of the runners. Sometimes runners have been replaced in a slightly different position so that two sets of marks may be seen under the drawer. One need only be suspicious if the runners and marks do not match, for this, like a clean interior, indicates a completely new drawer. There may, however, be secret drawers within the carcase, or small drawers, all with bright clean interiors and this is understandable as they are likely to have been used much less frequently. The wood at the bottom of a drawer is sometimes found split and this is a good sign as it is owing to shrinkage which results from age. Attention has been drawn to the fact that a good but not always conclusive pointer to the age of the drawer is the direction of the grain of the timber at the bottom—from back to front before about 1740, sideways after that date.

Alterations of the handles of drawers can easily be detected by looking inside the drawer to see if there are any holes left by former fastenings and by checking any tell-tale marks on the exterior (though these may have been obscured by new handles). Handles and back-plates, if genuinely old, should have smooth surfaces after constant dusting and rubbing, and never rough ones—a matter which can be quickly checked by running the fingers over the surface. Old back-plates should also have a tiny border of dirt just outside the metal which the cleaning materials have not quite been able to reach. Locks were often changed on drawers and cupboard doors, perhaps because the originals had become loose or inoperative, or because a more efficient type had been fitted. Replacements can be checked by seeing whether the new lock fits precisely into the space formerly occupied by the original. The lock may also be stamped with a name, possibly that of a nineteenth-century manufacturer. The nature of the metal is also important as steel and iron locks were, as a general rule, nailed to the wood and brass ones screwed. As nails were all hand-made their authenticity can be verified by their faceted and slightly arched heads beaten out by the hammer. Rust from the old nails can lead to staining of the wood round the nail hole. Like nails, screws on antique furniture were hand-made and lack the even flat top and regular length of machine-made screws (which did not appear until after 1850). All this, of course, is well known to fakers who collect old screws and screw them in water-filled holes so that they rust in. An old screw is thus no proof of age, but should it easily turn when tested with a screwdriver then it has obviously not been long in the wood.

Note has already been made of the frequent re-upholstering of old chairs. If the chair has a stuff-over seat, one which has its rails completely covered by upholstery, there will be plenty of holes in the wood of the rails to mark the places where successive sets of upholstery have been fastened on, for the upholsterer avoids previous tack holes when renewing the covers. The corner (or angle) blocks on chairs, the struts or brackets fixed in the inner angles of seat rails to reinforce the joints of the legs, were often, in the case of stuff-over chairs, pieces of wood let into notches cut in the top of the rails and subsequently hidden by the upholstery. Loose, drop-in seats, however, had triangular blocks screwed into the angles to give extra support to the seat, as well as to strengthen the joints. Lighter chairs of the Sheraton style had two glued blocks which were rounded off into a curve.

Tripod tables, the pillar and claws usually with round tops, are perhaps the most frequently 'married' pieces of furniture and need critical examination. The wood of the support should match that of the top, and even two different types of mahogany should arouse suspicion. The feet should project slightly beyond the line of the circumference of the top, otherwise the table will not be properly balanced; a top transferred from one support to another does not always meet this requirement. The age of a round top can be quickly gauged with a measuring tape. As wood shrinks across the grain in process of time, genuine tops will measure slightly less (about one-half to one-quarter inch) across than with the grain. A newly turned top will be an exact circle. Under the top there should be a narrow rim of dark marks made by generations of fingers moving the table. Larger tripods had plain circular edges. As such tables with fretted galleries round their tops, or with carved scalloped ('piecrust') edges, are rare and therefore command a high price today, fakers have often given plain tables (using the original wood) a gallery or carved edge. These are difficult to detect. Genuine galleries, however, were made of plywood of fret-cut veneers glued together for strength and so galleries of fretted solid mahogany are suspect at once. Also, if a mark such as a scratch on the top of the table continues under the gallery it is a sign that the latter has been added. Piecrust edges were cut in the solid by recessing the centre of the top and carving the undulating edge, a difficult task as the wood in places had to be carved against the grain, hence the high cost of such decoration. Plain table tops are not thick enough to leave sufficient wood to carve the edge and one therefore occasionally finds a shaped moulding applied to the outline, and the join can be detected.

Worm holes resembling those in old furniture can easily be faked. Sometimes, however, the faker oversteps the mark by boring holes right through the wood whereas the hole is the escape route for the grub which resides in a tunnel parallel to the wood's surface. Occasionally these tunnels are exposed when old wood has been cut through. They have been found, for example, on the side of a drawer in the central section of a Tudor court cupboard, proving, with other evidence, that the drawer had been made up of old wood and inserted later, probably in the nineteenth century. The unpolished wood on furniture, the normally unseen inner and bottom sections such as the inside of the seat rails of chairs and settees and the underframing of carcases and drawer linings is always worth investigation. Old unpolished wood, chiefly oak, beech and deal, employed for carcase work and as backing for veneers, has a dry and mature appearance which it is very difficult to counterfeit, unlike the polished surfaces of oak, walnut, mahogany, etc. which can be given the appearance of age without much trouble. If fakers could get sections of old beech beds which chairmakers of the past used to employ for their seat rails the task of counterfeiting would be much easier, but such old wood is now in very short supply. Attempts may be made to disguise new wood by staining it, a fact which should excite suspicion at once. As those stained parts are usually hidden from direct view they can be safely tested by slight chipping with a penknife, and new wood will appear white under the stain.

When veneered case furniture is under examination, the veneers should match all the way down and less attractive veneers are found on the sides of the piece. The colour of the veneers should also be the same throughout, but allowance must be made for fading if the furniture has stood for a long time in strong sunlight.

The so-called 'Elizabethan' revival of c. 1825 onwards often incorporated late Stuart features. This 'Elizabethan' chair of c. 1845 confirms this, with its spiral turning, framed back and cresting.

# Museums and Collections
# of English Furniture

For all those interested in antique English furniture—especially visitors to Britain—who wish to extend their knowledge there is great wealth of material for study, so much indeed, that in this short review of museums and collections references must necessarily be very selective. Two annual publications, *Museums and Galleries*, and *Historic Houses, Castles and Gardens*, provide information about collections of furniture throughout the United Kingdom. The places concerned are very conveniently grouped by locality, the museums by towns, and the historic houses by counties. A brief note is appended to each entry giving details of the contents, so that references to furniture collections can easily be traced. Armed with these publications, the enquiring collector can soon find what is available. There is something for every kind of interest, general or specialised. One can concentrate, for instance, on the furniture of a particular period, or on that associated with a famous designer or craftsman, such as Adam or Chippendale, or on the more modest furnishings of the smaller middle-class home, or on the country pieces intended for farmhouses and cottages.

Ideally, furniture should be studied in the setting for which it was originally made. This can be done in houses which have retained their furniture. There is special interest in those in which, over the centuries, successive owners have furnished new rooms or wings with currently fashionable pieces while preserving intact the older parts of the house and their contents. England is fortunate in having a number of houses where this is the case, Hardwick Hall, Derbyshire and Knole, Kent, being two famous examples. But inevitably collections of early furniture *in situ* are now rare, as old pieces have succumbed to wear and tear, or have been destroyed by fire, or have been discarded as being too old-fashioned.

Sometimes a museum will take over a furnished house, but

normally it differs from the 'stately home' of the kind described, in that its collection of furniture, specially gathered together with the object of stimulating interest and increasing knowledge, will be a comprehensive one (though specialist collections, of course, are to be found) and its success depends on the arrangement and presentation in its galleries. A wide variety of authorities in Britain own, control and administer the houses and museums that contain furniture collections. To take the houses, for instance, that are open to the public, such authorities include private individuals (in many cases they are descendants of the original owners, as at Hatfield House, Hertfordshire; Chatsworth, Derbyshire; Woburn Abbey, Bedfordshire; and Holkham Hall, Norfolk), government departments (the Ministry of Public Buildings and Works is responsible for Chiswick House, Middlesex and Osborne House, Isle of Wight), the National Trust (a voluntary body responsible for some 200 houses), museums (Osterley Park House, Middlesex and Ham House, Surrey, are both administered by the Victoria and Albert Museum), local authorities (who run, among many others, such famous houses as Aston Hall, Birmingham; Kenwood, London; and Temple Newsam House, Leeds), and, finally, a whole range of private companies, societies and schools. Whatever the character of their administration, all such houses are open to visitors, though their opening times and conditions of entry may vary considerably. Most of them issue illustrated booklets which are well worth collecting for their reference to and illustrations of furniture. But when a house has passed out of family possession into other hands, it may often be an empty shell because the contents have gone, perhaps to pay death duties. In this case it has to be furnished anew, and while this is done with care and discernment in most cases, the direct link between the house and its original contents has been lost, and naturally the amount, variety and quality of the furniture on view depend on the size, facilities and endowments of the house.

The finest collection of furniture in an English museum is that at the Victoria and Albert Museum, London. Here the furniture is so arranged that to walk through the galleries is to make a progress through English furniture history, from 1500 to 1914. As well as outstanding masterpieces of English joinery and cabinet-making there are representative middle-class pieces. At frequent intervals authentic period rooms, removed from their original buildings, have been carefully re-assembled in the galleries, complete with wall and ceiling decoration, and have been furnished in contemporary style, including lighting, clocks, mirrors and carpets. In many of these rooms the visitor is allowed free access so that their period atmosphere can be completely absorbed.

Another famous London museum, the Geffrye Museum, Shoreditch, has a similar arrangement of period rooms, from 1600 to the present, with appropriate furniture, but in this case the exhibits are from typical middle-class homes. Throughout Britain this presentation of period rooms has been adopted by museums, another well-known example being the Castle Museum, York.

Notable museum collections outside London, again to name only a few, can be seen at the Lady Lever Art Gallery, Port Sunlight; Temple Newsam House; Strangers' Hall, Norwich (illustrating urban domestic life); Christ Church Mansion, Ipswich; and Aston Hall. Smaller museums and houses tend to concentrate on representative merchants', local and country furniture. Thus a number of houses connected with Shakespeare in and around Stratford-on-Avon, administered by Shakespeare's Birthplace Trust Properties, have been carefully furnished with Tudor and Jacobean furniture of this kind. Sulgrave Manor, Northamptonshire, famous as the home of George Washington's ancestors, is a good example of a smaller manor house of the seventeenth century. Townend, Troutbeck, Westmorland, is a most interesting yeomen's house of the early seventeenth century which contains furniture made over three centuries by members of the same family, down to the death of the last of the male line in 1914.

There are, of course, a number of private collections not open to the public. Owners are generally reluctant to have their treasures inspected, naturally enough when one considers their value, especially of such articles as rare clocks. But there have been some good exhibitions in recent years when furniture from such collections has been on view, including royal pieces. The catalogues of these exhibitions well repay study (many are still available for purchase in some cases) and exceptional recent examples include *English Taste in the Eighteenth Century* (Royal Academy, 1955–56), *The Orange and The Rose: Holland and Britain in the Age of Observation, 1600–1750* (1964), and *The British Antique Dealer's Golden Jubilee Exhibition* (1968), these last two being held at the Victoria and Albert Museum. A successful specialist exhibition, *101 Chairs*, held in Oxford in 1968, has an annotated illustrated catalogue (see under Bibliography). In 1971 Temple Newsam House staged an exhibition of regional furniture (from Yorkshire churches), a pioneer attempt to study the regional characteristics of English furniture, a much neglected subject.

Antique dealers' fairs are now held in every part of the country, a striking proof of the ever-growing interest in antiques. The major event of this kind is the Antique Dealers' Fair and Exhibition, held every summer at Grosvenor House, London. This fair specialises in the best material for sale in the antiques world and issues a lavishly illustrated catalogue. Such fairs give the visitor information about the current prices of antique furniture though the goods on show are specially selected to tempt buyers.

For a study of the initial stages in furniture-making in the past—to show how the timber was prepared, what tools were used and what other equipment could be found in joiners' and cabinet-makers' workshops—some museums have collected implements of all kinds. The City Museum, St. Albans, displays a reconstructed saw-pit and also contains the fine Salaman Collection of woodworking tools. The cells in the old Debtors' Prison which is adjacent to the Castle Museum, York, have been turned into a fascinating series of craft workshops, including those dealing with every aspect of woodworking. Rural furniture-making is dealt with in the Museum of English Rural Life, University of Reading, and

81

the Windsor chair is the appropriate theme of the Art Gallery and Museum, High Wycombe, where there is another excellent exhibition of craftsmen's tools.

Britain has been fortunate in having the only American museum outside the United States. This is at Claverton, near Bath, where American furniture, with other crafts, is displayed in a series of furnished rooms. The furniture, dating from colonial days, makes a most interesting subject for comparison with contemporary English furniture. The famous open-air Welsh Folk Museum at St. Fagan's Castle, Cardiff, will provide further interesting comparative study with its displays of Welsh furniture and rural crafts.

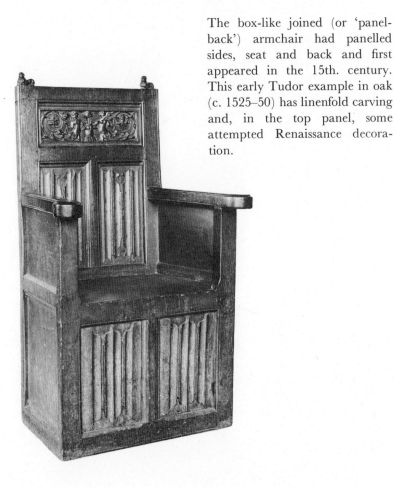

The box-like joined (or 'panel-back') armchair had panelled sides, seat and back and first appeared in the 15th. century. This early Tudor example in oak (c. 1525–50) has linenfold carving and, in the top panel, some attempted Renaissance decoration.

# PART 2

The growing sophistication of furniture in the Jacobean period is seen in this cabinet of c. 1600–25. While the outside is painted black, the interior has gilded and silvered *chinoiserie* decoration. The stand is later.

By the beginning of the 17th. century the early Tudor panel-back chair had shed its side and seat panels and had incorporated 'head' and 'ear' pieces. It was now possible to turn the front legs and arm supports and to curve the arms. This example shows fashionable late Tudor decoration, derived from northern Europe, of inlaid floral and chequer ornament.

The long fixed dining table ('table dormant'), produced by the joiner, was a prominent feature in large early Tudor households. This is a typical example of the period, with turned legs of baluster form.

This type of chest was very popular in Elizabethan England and has been given the name 'Nonesuch' from the supposed resemblance of its inlaid decoration to Henry VII's Palace of Nonesuch, Cheam, Surrey. Almost certainly, however, such chests were imported from Germany (or made in England by immigrant craftsmen).

A light version of the panel-back chair came into use c. 1525–50 for bedrooms and parlours. This was the caquetoire or conversation chair. It had a narrow back and widely splayed arms and was open beneath the arms and seat. The example shown is French, or an English version of a French type, and is made of walnut.

Small portable desks had obvious advantages. This example of the late 16th. century is fitted with a nest of drawers. It has inlaid chequer ornament and representations of a building similar to those on Nonesuch chests and bedheads.

With the development of a separate dining room for family use arose the need for the draw table which could be extended to double its length for meals. This early example, which has a panelled top and dates from the first half of the 16th. century, has a most attractive simple functional form.

This oak draw table of c. 1600 incorporates the typical Elizabethan
decoration of bulbous legs and inlaid chequer patterns of sycamore, bog
oak and other woods.

The sloping top has become a traditional feature of furniture intended for reading. Its medieval ancestry is clearly seen in this rare early example (perhaps late 15th. century) of a desk carved with Gothic arcading.

This early example of a chest of drawers is dated 1653. The upper stage has a shallow drawer in the frieze and a deep drawer; the lower stage has three long drawers behind the panelled doors. The mouldings and inlay, which include bone and ivory as well as woods, indicate foreign, probably Dutch, influence.

Gate-leg tables served many purposes in the early 17th. century. This side table has a folding top which can be hinged back and supported on a gate-leg. The opened top makes a complete circle and the lower flap of the top forms the lid of a semicircular box within the frieze.

The chest remained important long after losing its medieval predominance. This oak example of the 17th. century retains its original hinges; the mouldings on the front panels are cut from the solid, and split balusters decorate the stiles.

The joined ('joynt') stool with four turned legs appeared in the late 16th. century. Note how the pegs securing the joints are clearly visible, a piece of revealed construction which became fashionable again three centuries later.

A type of chair without arms, introduced in the 16th. century, was known to contemporaries as a 'back stool'. This example in oak, of c. 1625–50, has been given the modern name of 'farthingale chair' as its wide seat was supposed to be designed for ladies wearing the fashionable farthingale dress.

A light folding chair was popular in the late 16th century. Its modern name of 'Glastonbury' chair appears to derive from Henry Shaw's Specimens of Ancient Furniture, 1836, in which an example is described as the "Abbot's chair, Glastonbury," and incorrectly dated to Henry VIII's reign. Our illustration shows the round arches and enclosed lozenge carving of the early 17th century.

The earliest type of walnut chair to appear in Charles II's reign was
· admirably simple and well-proportioned, as this example of c. 1660 shows.
It has spirally turned uprights, legs and stretchers, and cane seat and back.

By the late 17th. century the chest of drawers had finally evolved from the medieval chest. This example of c. 1675–1700 is decorated with panels of floral marquetry set against parquetry of oyster pieces. The base is later.

The gate-leg table continued to serve many useful purposes. By c. 1660 it had two elliptical flaps which were supported by a gate-leg on either side of the rectangular centre panel.

This chest of drawers of 1670–80 aptly demonstrates the post-1660 revolution in constructional and decorative techniques. Its exterior is decorated with floral marquetry, the interior with parquetry of oyster pieces. Such pieces were made to contain collections of valuable 'curiosities.'

Towards the end of the 17th. century cabinets were supported on chests of drawers in preference to stands. This William and Mary cabinet (c. 1690) is of kingwood decorated with parquetry of walnut oyster pieces; it has bun feet, cross-banding on the drawer fronts and lip moulding at the top of the underframe.

This magnificent cabinet on chest of drawers was made c. 1700 for a marriage between the Lawson and Trotter families of Yorkshire. The walnut veneer is decorated with marquetry of ivory, mother-of-pearl, sycamore, ash and other woods.

Eaton Hall
College of Education Library

The late Stuart craze for *chinoiseries* resulted in English imitation of oriental lacquered cabinets. This English example was made in the last quarter of the 17th. century. It is japanned in bright colours, including gold and silver, on a black ground, and has an elaborate carved and silvered stand.

English writing cabinets based on French prototypes were known as 'scriptors'. They had a large fall-front and were supported on stands. Ham House, near Richmond, has celebrated examples, of which this is one, made c. 1675, and veneered with kingwood oyster pieces.

Another Ham House scriptor has burr walnut veneers and is embossed with silver mounts. Its stand is carved and partly silvered. Made c. 1675, these Ham House scriptors appear in an inventory of the house drawn up in 1679.

By the end of Charles II's reign (1685) the chair back had become taller and more slender although retaining much of its former elaboration.

Reaction against Puritanism and increasing love of luxury led to elaborate decoration of furniture in Charles II's reign of which this chair of c. 1680 is a good example. It has lavishly carved back panel, cresting and front stretcher, spirally turned uprights, and scrolled front legs and arm supports.

Graceful simplicity re-asserted itself under William & Mary (1689–1702). This painted beech chair of c. 1695 has its slender back accentuated by the baluster turned uprights. The carved cresting matches the front stretcher.

Upholstered chairs avoided much of the elaboration of Carolean walnut cane chairs. This armchair, made for Ham House c. 1675, has gracefully turned legs, arms and arm supports.

The fashionable late Stuart passion for card games produced the first specially made card tables. This table of c. 1700, of Italian walnut, has a half oval folding top which opens on gate-leg supports. Shapely turned legs are a feature of this period.

*Chinoiseries* continued to fascinate English craftsmen. This is a cabinet of c. 1715 made mainly of Japanese lacquer on an English gilt gesso stand which closely resembles a side table at Hampton Court made by the royal cabinet-maker, James Moore.

TOP

The attractive simplicity of walnut furniture comes out clearly in this chest of drawers of the early 18th. century. The framework has a half-round moulding. It has a folding top for writing, supported on two pull-out slides.

BOTTOM

The simple type of writing desk on stand enjoyed a vogue well into the 18th. century. Here the sloping top is supported on the two inner legs which swing forward on hinges. The arabesque marquetry, fashionable in the early 1700s, is either Dutch or English.

The early 18th. century bureau-cabinet showed a masterly command of good proportions. This example is decorated with burr walnut veneers and its arched top, echoed by mouldings on the doors, displays Baroque influence.

This is an unusual example of a bureau-cabinet made in oak. Here the dwarf cabriole legs have replaced bun, ball or bracket feet, the cornice is straight and the door has an arched moulding. This may well be the work of a competent provincial maker.

The walnut period produced comfortable seat furniture as this settee ('love seat') of c. 1715 shows. The walnut cabriole legs are parcel (i.e. partly) gilt. The deep upholstery and scrolled arms add to comfort without adversely affecting good design.

The simple dignity of late walnut furniture is exemplified in this knee-hole pedestal dressing table of c. 1710, with beautifully figured veneers.

The wing armchair, intended for family rooms, has become the classic English easy chair. In the early Georgian period it was made (as here) in mahogany and adopted the short cabriole leg with claw-and-ball foot.

Seating furniture became notably wider in the second quarter of the 18th. century to accommodate the more voluminous costume worn by both men and women. The leather on this mahogany example of c. 1740 has been renewed.

The chair constructed of turned members (said to be 'turned all over') has a very long history. For centuries it was a stock cottage chair, and continued to be made on traditional lines, as this chair dated 1718 shows, well after the arrival of more sophisticated types.

The curvilinear chair, with its superb mastery of controlled and contrasted curves, was a notable advance in English chair design. This superb example of c. 1730, veneered on the uprights, splat and seat rails, with delicately carved cabriole legs and cresting, marks perhaps the height of the achievement of the walnut period.

The chest on chest (or 'tallboy') was a popular 18th. century piece. It lent itself to a fine display of veneers as seen in this example of c. 1720–30, which has a writing slide in the lower stage. The top drawers, however, were awkward to get at and the piece went out of fashion by 1800.

English japanners had a near-monopoly of the home market when the government raised import duties on imported lacquer in 1701. This pine bureau-bookcase of c. 1720–40 has brilliant japanned decoration of red and gold. The broken arched pediment and bracket feet are very typical of the period.

The bureau completes its development when the desk with sloping top is added to the chest of drawers, and the result is a pleasing union of function and good proportions. This bureau of c. 1725 has its oak and pine carcase veneered with walnut, yew and amboyna.

This bureau of c. 1730–40 shows the tendency to elaboration of the early part of George II's reign. The base of carved walnut and the carved paw feet add touches of fussiness.

The most graceful form of the cabriole leg is undoubtedly that seen on early 18th. century card and side tables. This card table of c. 1720, of carved walnut and walnut veneers, has a hinged top which is supported by swinging out one of the legs.

Mahogany brought additional properties of strength and therefore slenderness (as well as crisp carving) to furniture. This mahogany side table, made c. 1725, has a drawer and writing slide in the frieze, and unusual brass inlay on the top.

There continued to be a vogue for simpler types of looking-glasses. This
mirror of c. 1740 has a moulded frame of veneered walnut and a central
carved and gilt shell sunk in cresting and base.

Large open fires in Georgian houses could sometimes be uncomfortably hot, hence the use of fire screens. This walnut cheval screen of c. 1740 has a finely carved cresting centring in a shell, and a needlework panel.

The pillar and claw table was a most useful piece, especially for serving tea; hence the scalloped ('piecrust') edge to prevent the precious tea things from being too easily swept off. This tripod of c. 1750 in mahogany has a hinged top.

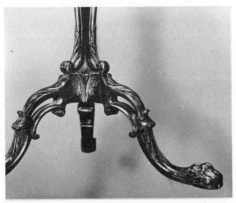

The fine precision of carved mahogany comes out clearly in this detail of the base of a tripod stand (or 'pillar and claw') with hairy paw feet. c. 1750.

Mahogany's carving qualities encouraged a certain amount of exhibitionism, inevitable also in a reaction against former simplicity. This George II side table (c. 1750) has a carved mask in the centre of the frieze and hoof feet set off by carved hair.

It is necessary to note that walnut continued in fashionable use for some time after the advent of mahogany. This walnut bureau, for instance, with fine burr veneers, was made c. 1750, and is very unusual in bearing the trade label of Elizabeth Bell & Son of St. Paul's Churchyard, London.

This early Georgian long-case clock is veneered with burr ash and has an unusual combination of pediment and arched dial.

This mahogany china cabinet of c. 1750 reflects the architectural approach of William Kent (d. 1748) with its pediment, side brackets and carved key pattern. Yet the beginnings of rococo reaction can be seen in the delicately carved floral pendants.

This armchair of c. 1750 marks the transition between baroque and rococo. It may well have been a 'pattern chair', i.e. a mode· for craftsmen and a guide to clients, as it has five different designs on its legs, seat and arms.

The serpentine front of this bureau dressing table of c. 1750, the asymmetrical handles and the design of other mounts all denote the rococo approach which affected furniture design after 1750. The brass work on this piece strongly suggests the work of John Channon, known to have been influenced by German designs.

The subtle serpentine line of the front, the carved angle trusses and base and the handles of this mahogany chest of drawers of c. 1760 all denote the impact of rococo taste on English case furniture.

This commode formerly at Badminton House was for long ascribed to Chippendale, but is now known to have been made by William Linnell, c. 1753–54. Japanned in black and gold, it employs Chinese lattice work and has a rococo serpentine front.

As a concession to francophile clients, the *Director* included designs for 'ribband back' chairs one of which was the model for the example illustrated here. Despite the virtuosity of the carving, the elaboration is too French for English taste.

As this mahogany armchair very closely resembles a design in Chippendale's *Director* of 1754 it can justifiably be taken to typify the anglicised version of the rococo with its masterly controlled use of C and S scrolls.

The revived interest in *chinoiseries* marked in Chippendale's *Director* was allied to the metallic strength of mahogany to produce attractive small pieces. This cabinet on stand of c. 1750 is decorated with tortoiseshell, ivory and delicately carved trellis work.

Kent's monumental side tables were too grand for general English taste, but the Chippendale period continued to indulge in stately pieces of this kind. Here is an example with carved and gilt festoons of flowers on the frieze centring in acanthus. The top is of marble.

The mahogany break-front bookcase was the principal feature of English libraries. The fretted gallery top and carved finials were characteristic features c. 1760.

The asymmetry which was a tenet of rococo carving is clearly portrayed in this cheval fire screen of c. 1755, with mahogany frame and 'knurl' feet (taken directly from French models). The panel is of needlework.

The attractive lightness of tea furniture is beautifully conveyed in this urn stand of c. 1760. It has cluster column legs, crossed stretchers and fretted gallery.

This is a typically 'Chippendale' piece in its interpretation of *chinoiseries*. It is of mahogany, with card cut lattice ornament on the frieze and fretted bracket. It is also a late version of the desk on stand, for the upper desk, which has a side drawer and adjustable top, also has handles for lifting clear of the table.

131

This armchair is the type described in Chippendale's *Director* as a 'French elbow chair'. Its gilt framework is carved in rococo taste and is 'open at the back', i.e. has a space between the back and the rear seat rail. The date is c. 1760.

Another example of 'Chinese Chippendale'—a tea table of mahogany of c. 1755, with Chinese frets, open or closed, on the gallery, frieze, legs and brackets.

Chinese frets are the dominant theme of this 'Chinese Chippendale' armchair of c. 1760, which also has a typical pagoda cresting.

The Kimbolton cabinet, a magnificent example of English neo-classical furniture, was made to display eleven marble intarsia panels for the Duchess of Manchester at Kimbolton Castle. It was designed by Robert Adam in 1771 and made by Ince and Mayhew of London. The ormolu mounts came from Boulton and Fothergill of Birmingham.

By 1770 neo-classical taste had begun to affect chair design as this example shows. Its oval back with frame decorated with swags of husks, the serpentine rail with rosettes, and the straight tapered legs of round section with spiral reeding all illustrate the impact of the new style.

TOP

The great skill of English craftsmen in the revived marquetry of the neo-classical period is evident in the detail of the front of the commode.

BOTTOM

This exquisite small commode of 1770–75 has the serpentine front and sides and bombé shape of its French prototypes, in rococo taste. The decoration, however, of mahogany with marquetry panels and borders, is incipient neo-classical. This superb piece closely resembles work by John Cobb, the royal cabinet-maker.

French influence on English furniture remained strong. This carved mahogany armchair of c. 1765 is based directly on French models and retains the lightness and grace of the rococo phase.

The increasing delicacy of furniture reached almost fragile proportions towards the end of the 18th. century, with portability a decisive consideration. This writing cabinet on a slender stand, made c. 1775–80, is of satinwood with oval panels of amboyna or burr walnut.

The late 18th. century bookcase made great play with the break-front, beautiful mahogany veneers and slender glazing bars of diverse forms.

Bookcases of smaller proportions at the end of the century—this Sheraton
period example was made c. 1795—used short tapered feet.

The graceful outward-curving feet and shaped apron of this chest of drawers indicate a date of c. 1770–80. The serpentine front shows off the brilliant mahogany figure.

English neo-classical chair design set the fashion for the rest of Europe. One of its greatest contributions was the famous shield-back which was popularised by Hepplewhite (though he did not initiate it). This example has a carved wheat sheaf in its mahogany shield frame, and characteristic straight tapered legs. c. 1785.

By the end of the century chairs began to revert to square backs in reaction
to the diverse round, oval, heart and shield shapes favoured by neo-
classical designers. This chair, with vertical bars filling the back, resembles
(but does not imitate) a design in Hepplewhite's *Guide* of 1794, third
edition, which itself was obviously influenced by the square backs in
Sheraton's *Drawing Book* of 1791–4.

Neo-classical taste reigns supreme in this satinwood bureau-bookcase of c. 1780, decorated with patterned material in the upper oval panels, and with marquetry, carving and painted ornament.

Simple, dignified proportions were the keynotes of library table design.
This example, probably made in the mid 1780s, resembles a design in
Hepplewhite's *Guide* (1788) and incorporates enamel plaques. Mahogany
remained the supreme wood for all library furniture.

Marquetry in French fashion distinguishes this commode of c. 1780.

Few pieces of English furniture have combined utility and elegance more aptly than Hepplewhite period sideboards. This bow-fronted sideboard of c. 1790, with central drawer flanked by two cupboards, and tapered legs on plinth feet (four in front and two behind) represents English craftsmanship at its peak.

The dumb waiter became a standard feature of the Georgian dining room. The curved feet of this two-tiered mahogany waiter denote a late 18th. century date.

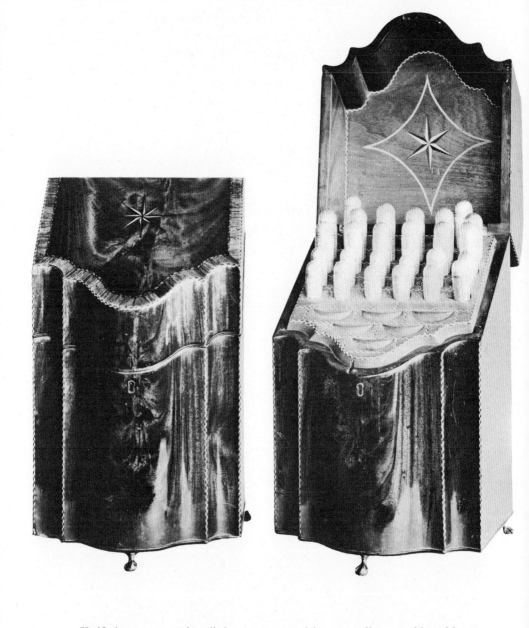

Knife boxes were also dining room requisites, standing on side tables or sideboards. These two examples clearly show their attractive shape and decoration.

The refinements of c. 1790 are clearly illustrated in this bureau-bookcase with slender shaped feet, curved apron, cylinder bureau top, Gothic glazing bars and stamped brass handles.

This late 18th. century commode has a convex centre of three drawers flanked by concave cupboards. The wood is satinwood with rosewood cross-binding, and the floral swags and vases of flowers are painted.

One of the newer types of table to appear c. 1800 was the sofa table, a slightly longer version of the Pembroke table. As its name implies, it was conveniently placed near a sofa. This shows an early example in mahogany.

The refined simplicity associated with the designs of Sheraton is exemplified in this two-tiered writing cabinet with cylinder desk of c. 1795 (though it does not follow a specific Sheraton drawing). It is decorated with beautiful mahogany veneers, painted panels and Wedgwood plaques (within the writing top).

Of even more delicate beauty is this lady's portable writing cabinet
veneered in Cuban mahogany on slender tapered legs. c. 1795.

Another example of a portable writing table with cylinder top is of mahogany with stringing decoration and a small brass gallery. It can be dated to c. 1800.

The bureau adopted the cylinder top, one of the discoveries of the late 18th. century. This version, raised by tapered legs above floor level, has amboyna wood veneers, in the current fashion for speckled wood of "bird's-eye" figure.

This mahogany centre table was probably made right at the end of the 18th. century. Its four swept legs united by a platform forecast the Regency fondness for round tables.

Regency designers were intrigued by the straight lines and compact scale of the furniture of antiquity. They also employed much brass—its durability and cheapness had special appeal in the stringency imposed by the French Wars, 1793–1815. This satinwood cabinet, only a little above four feet high, has brass trellis doors backed by pleated silk, ebony stringing and a painted panel.

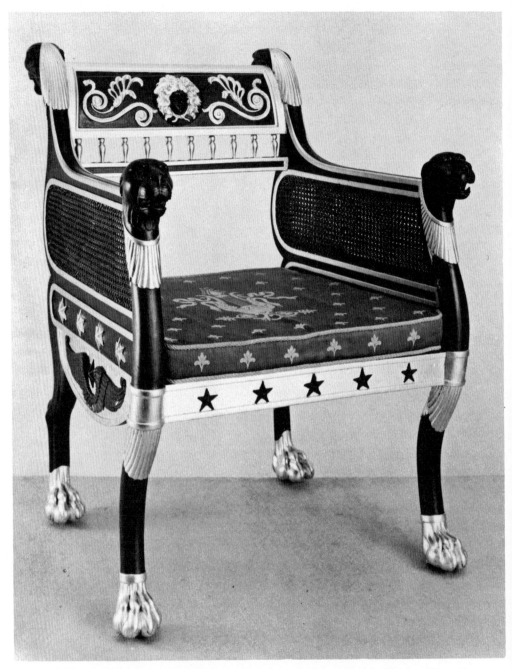

In full Regency Egyptian taste, this chair, painted black with gilt ornaments, was probably made in 1806 from a design dated 1804 and subsequently published in George Smith's *Household Furniture*, 1808.

This mahogany 'Gothick' chair was made c. 1823 for Eaton Hall, Cheshire. It is essentially a standard type of chair with Gothic trimmings.

Games tables, usually incorporating requisites for several games, resulted in the production of portable, elegant and well-equipped furniture. This is an example of the early 19th. century.

Concave ('sabre') front legs were distinguishing features of Regency chairs, as were also lion paw feet, exhibited in this painted and gilt chair of c. 1805.

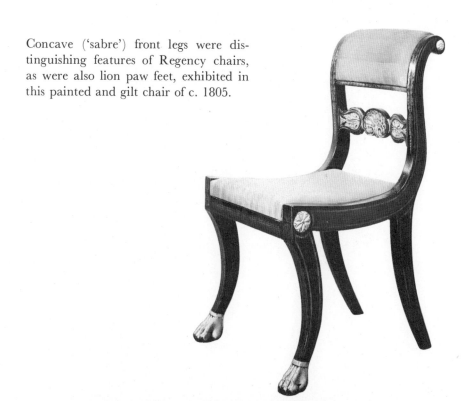

A view of the interior of the premises of Morgan and Sanders (c. 1810) of Catherine Street, off the Strand. The firm called their premises "Trafalgar House" as they had supplied furniture to Nelson.

As well as compactness and straight lines, Regency designers loved dark, glossy and striped woods to set off bright metal mounts and borders and inlay of light-coloured woods. This early 19th. century secretaire is of mahogany veneered with zebra wood and cross-banded with satinwood, and it incorporates Egyptian heads.

Dwarf furniture followed strict classical precedents and also left the wall above free for hanging pictures. This bookcase is typical of this trend and was probably made c. 1810.

Circular and oval tables were in favour during the Regency. This oval
table with mahogany tip-up top, has characteristic curved legs and brass
paws.

This rosewood side table with ormolu mounts, marble top and supports in Egyptian taste is another typical piece of c. 1810. It also exhibits strong French influence, reflecting the strict classical Empire style cultivated by Napoleon.

This unusual display table exhibits many characteristic Regency features—
rosewood veneers, mirror back, S-scroll side supports, tapered reeded legs,
lotus leaf ornament on the upper legs, a brass gallery and brass column
supports to the shelf.

This Regency sofa table, of amboyna and kingwood veneers, with brass inlay, gilt brass mounts and a central pedestal on four curved legs, matches three other tables which were made for Princess Charlotte in 1816.

Boulle marquetry furniture had a fashionable revival in England after 1800. This commode of c. 1820 has boulle panels and gilt brass ornament on a rosewood ground.

This mahogany Davenport (named after the client whom Gillows supplied with the prototype) has a sloping desk top and drawers and slide at the side. The other side has dummy drawer fronts to match. This was to become a favourite writing desk in the Victorian period.

The Canterbury was a small stand with racks to hold music books, very fashionable after 1800.

There is no mistaking the typical Regency mirror—convex glass, gilt cavetto moulding with gilt balls, inner ebonised and reeded fillet (or slip) and surmounting eagle with balls suspended from its beak on a chain.

Early 19th. century features seen on this bureau-cabinet are the outward curving feet and shaped apron, lion handles with ring, and the figured veneers within the oval mouldings on the cupboard doors.

In spite of the skill shown in the marquetry (which is composed of various woods, including rosewood, maple and kingwood on a mahogany carcase) and parquetry, this writing desk of c. 1830 clearly demonstrates that the archaeological precision of the Regency is on the wane.

This 'Grecian' table of c. 1830, made of burr walnut and maple, with boulle decoration, continued as a fashionable piece into the Victorian period.

This fine example of a "Grecian" dining chair of mahogany, with leather seat and back rest, was designed in 1834 by the architect Philip Hardwick for Goldsmiths' Hall.

One of the Victorian achievements in chair design was the balloon-back. These two examples illustrate the penultimate and final forms of this type, of c. 1830 (with heavy forms of cabriole legs) and of c. 1850 (when the rounded back is balanced by slender cabrioles).

This oak armchair with imitation leather was designed by A. W. N. Pugin and made by J. G. Crace for Scarisbrick Hall c. 1837. It illustrates again Pugin's clear grasp of Gothic principles.

We must abandon once and for all the notion that Victorian furniture was inevitably over-elaborate. This attractive 'fly' chair, of beech carved, painted and gilded, was designed by Philip Hardwick and made by Wilkinson c. 1834 for Goldsmith's Hall.

A. W. N. Pugin was the first Victorian designer to produce Gothic furniture based on sound knowledge and understanding. This cabinet designed by Pugin for Abney Hall, Cheshire, c. 1847, has real feeling for Gothic form, construction and decoration, and does not merely add Gothic ornament to current furniture.

The loo table (named after a popular card-game) was a very fashionable
type in the Victorian period. This example of c. 1850, on a central column
with three legs, has typical carved decoration. The unusual decoration of
the top has inset metal plaques on a blue velvet ground.

Most people would associate this type of chair without hesitation with the early Victorian period. Made c. 1845, it is upholstered in Berlin wool-work and derives its curves from a version of the Louis XIV style.

Two unmistakable Victorian features are illustrated in this chair of c. 1840— its shape, the 'prie-dieu', another distinct contribution to chair design, and its material, papier mâché, usually japanned black and decorated with painting or mother-of-pearl.

This papier máché half tester bed of c. 1850 actually has an iron structure to which the papier mâché head and footboards, painted and gilt, are added.

With the foundation of Morris & Co. in 1861, Pugin's pioneer work was taken a stage further when simple functional furniture, such as these chairs of c. 1865, based on English vernacular types, was produced by the firm.

# Glossary of Technical Terms

*Acanthus*   Stylised leaf of classical architecture frequently found as carved decoration, especially on late seventeenth and eighteenth century furniture.

*Amorini*   Cupids carved on post-Restoration furniture, especially chairs.

*Anthemion*   Stylised honeysuckle of classical origin, often found carved, inlaid and painted on Adam and Regency furniture; also alternating with palmette (q.v.).

*Apron piece*   Ornamental rail on underframing of chests of drawers, etc., and between tops of legs of tables and chairs.

*Arabesque*   Ornament of foliate, scrolls and geometric patterns, fancifully interpreting Islamic designs, found in 'seaweed' marquetry from c. 1690 and on gesso tables c. 1690–1730.

*Astragal*   Semicircular moulding at junction of doors to exclude dust; also general term for late Georgian glazing bars.

*Ball foot*   Spherical base of turned leg on late seventeenth-century furniture.

*Baluster*   Spiral, straight, vase-shaped, etc. turned column.

*Banding*   Decorative border on veneered furniture.

*Baroque*   Bold and somewhat florid version of Renaissance decoration prevalent in late seventeenth century and particularly in the carved and gilt furniture of William Kent, c. 1725–50.

*Bead*   Small moulding of semicircular section or resembling string of beads; a variant, the bead and reel, used round and oblong forms.

*Bevel*   Angled cutting of edge of (usually) a panel or mirror.

*Bolection moulding*   Moulding of ogee (q.v.) section projecting round the edges of panels.

*Bombé*   Outward-swelling shape of furniture, a term adopted in England from France and applied especially to English commodes in the French taste.

*Boulle*   Inlay in tortoiseshell, brass and wood made famous by Louis XIV's *ébéniste*, A. C. Boulle (1642–1732); first produced in England by Gerreit Jensen at end of seventeenth century and revived during the Regency Period.

*Bracket foot* Of square shape, used on case furniture from c. 1690.

*Bulb* Swollen section of turned support on Elizabethan and Jacobean furniture, sometimes of 'cup and cover' form.

*Bun foot* Flattened form of ball foot.

*Cabochon* Convex oval ornament or jewel form in use from the Tudor Period and particularly on the knees of cabriole legs c. 1740.

*Card cut* Carved lattice ornament in low relief much used on Chippendale's 'Chinese' furniture.

*Cartouche* Ornament, originally a scroll of paper, oval in shape, enclosing a coat of arms, etc., and often in the centre of a broken pediment.

*Cavetto* Concave cornice moulding, especially in walnut period.

*Chamfer* Smoothed edge or bevelled angle; also described as canted or splayed.

*Channelling* Fluting (grooves) in stiles of oak furniture and in frames of Hepplewhite period chairs.

*Chinoiserie* Decoration inspired by Chinese taste, seen in japanned furniture, Chippendale's 'Chinese' designs, bamboo turning, etc.

*Chip carving* Shallow ornament worked with chisel and gouge on oak furniture.

*Claw-and-ball foot* Famous terminal of later walnut and earlier mahogany cabriole legs, derived from oriental motif of a jewel grasped in a dragon's claw.

*Club foot* Like the head of a club; the usual terminal of the cabriole leg and known as the pad foot when set on a disc.

*Cock bead* Small astragal moulding projecting from the edges of drawer fronts, c. 1730–1800.

*Console* 1, a bracket, normally scrolled and 2, a table introduced from France in the early eighteenth century, supported against the wall by front legs only, or by single support, e.g., a spread eagle.

*Cornice*   Projecting moulded member at the top of a book-case, cabinet or other tall piece of furniture.

*Cup and cover*   See BULB.

*Cupid's bow*   Modern name of the curved cresting rail of chairs from c. 1730, particularly applied to rococo chairs of the Chippendale period.

*Dentil*   'Tooth' moulding of small rectangular blocks often found on the cornices of mahogany furniture.

*Dolphin*   Ornament borrowed from France and used as a terminal on furniture, e.g., on the arms and feet of chairs in the late seventeenth century and again in the Kent and Chippendale periods.

*Dowel*   Wooden peg used for joining timber and widely used in the oak period.

*Ebonised wood*   A cheap wood (e.g. beech) stained black to imitate ebony and used as stringing in the late Georgian period.

*Egg and dart*   Classical ornament, supposed to symbolise life and death, often found carved on ovolo (q.v.) mouldings.

*Egyptian Taste*   Especially fashionable after 1798 (Napoleon's conquest of Egypt, Nelson's victory at the Nile) in the form of sphinx heads, lotus leaves, bolts, lions' heads, etc. found on Regency furniture.

*Escutcheon*   Shield of armorial bearings used as central ornament in broken pediments of case furniture; also the name of the ornamental metal plate round a keyhole.

*Fielded panel*   With its centre raised to project beyond the frame, or with its edges bevelled.

*Finial*   Ornament, often of vase-shape, at the corner of a pediment, on the tops of case furniture, clocks and pole screens, and also on the platform at the intersection of stretchers on late seventeenth-century tables and chairs.

*Fluting*   Channelled grooves decorating furniture from the sixteenth century on.

*French scroll*   Outward scrolling leg terminal of the rococo period; opposite of the inward turning knurl foot.

*Frets*   Repeated decorative patterns in the solid (see CARD CUT), found on the 'Chinese' furniture of the Chippendale era; or perforated, as in the galleries of tea tables.

*Frieze*   The horizontal section below the cornice of cabinets, etc., and the tops of tables.

*Gadrooning*   Edging of lobed (concave) repeated ornament much used in the oak period, e.g., on bulbs, and also after 1750; also known as 'nulling'.

*Gesso*   Composition of chalk and parchment size used as the base for gilding.

*Glazing bar*   Wooden members in windows, doors of book-cases, cabinets, etc. framing the glass panes.

*Greek key*   See KEY PATTERN.

*Guilloche*   Interlaced bands or ribbons, circles or ovals, sometimes enclosing rosettes or similar motifs, used as a border on sixteenth-century furniture and in the later Georgian Period.

*Herring bone banding*   A border of narrow strips of veneer laid in arrow-head formation, much used in the walnut period.

*Hipping*   Upward extension of the cabriole leg to the seat rail found on chairs and settees c. 1700–50.

*Hoof foot*   An early terminal to the cabriole leg, late seventeenth century.

*Husks*   Bell-shaped flowers in festoons, a very characteristic decoration on Adam and Hepplewhite furniture.

*Inlay*   Surface decoration with cuts or grooves within the wooden ground filled (to a depth of about one-eighth inch) with contrasting woods, mother-of-pearl, ivory or metal; differing from the surface decoration of veneering, but sometimes loosely used to describe the neo-classic marquetry of the Adam period.

*Key pattern*   Frieze ornament of classical derivation of repeated lines at right angles, particularly fashionable in the Kent period.

*Knurl foot*   The opposite of French scroll (q.v.).

*Linenfold*   Modern term for the panel decoration of Flemish origin in use c. 1480–1550; parchment or serviette pattern.

*Lion mask*   Carved lion's head favoured in the early mahogany period (c. 1725–40), particularly on knees of cabriole legs; also very popular motif of the Regency, e.g., for drawer handles.

*Lotus* Egyptian motif (currently known as the 'water lily of the Nile') of the Regency.

*Lozenge* Diamond-shaped moulded decoration of the Jacobean period especially on panels.

*Lunette* Half-moon shaped repeated decoration used as carved motif on later oak furniture, and inlaid or painted in Adam period.

*Mitre* Moulding intersection at corners of panels, each edge at an angle of 45°.

*Monopodium* Classical animal head and body with single foot, fashionable for table and chair legs in the Regency.

*Mortise* The recess in a piece of wood made to take the projecting tenon in another, the resulting joint creating 'joined' furniture made by the joiner.

*Neo-classical* The revived classicism of the post-1760 period usually with reference to Robert Adam's influence c. 1760–90, but also extending into the Regency Period to include the archaeological interpretation of classicism.

*Nulling* See GADROONING.

*Ogee* A waved moulding, convex above, concave below.

*Ormolu* Brass or bronze coated with an amalgam of mercury and gold dust then fired to a very high temperature. Imported from France until its manufacture in England by Matthew Boulton after 1762.

*Ovolo* A convex moulding found on drawer fronts in the late seventeenth century, in the form of a quarter round or ellipse.

*Oyster pieces* Small oval veneers cut from the branches of walnut, laburnum and olive trees to make geometrical patterns of parquetry after 1660.

*Palmette* Ornament derived from the date palm resembling a spread fan and very similar to the anthemion (q.v.).

*Papier mâché* A material patented by Henry Clay in 1772, but its use for furniture-making c. 1825–50 is based on its manufacture by a different process.

*Parquetry* See OYSTER PIECES.

*Patera*  Classical circular or oval motif much used in the Adam Period.

*Pediment*  Classical triangular section surmounting the cornice, e.g., on cabinets and bookcases; the 'broken' pediment with central space was fashionable in the eighteenth century.

*Piecrust*  The modern name for the raised scalloped edge of tea tables, c. 1750–75.

*Pier*  The solid part of the wall in a room between windows; hence pier table and pier glass.

*Pilaster*  Architectural term for a flat column of the classical orders; used on furniture from the sixteenth century, but very prevalent in the eighteenth as carved decoration. Brass pilasters are found on Regency furniture.

*Pillar and claw*  The contemporary term for a tripod table of three feet supporting a turned pillar; also known as a 'claw' table.

*Plinth*  The base of carcase furniture; also the spade foot at the base of the tapered leg of Hepplewhite chairs.

*Rail*  The horizontal member of a piece of furniture, particularly of a frame or door.

*Rebate*  The recess on the edge of a door or drawer to form a joint or receive another part.

*Reeding*  The convex raised ornament (in contrast to the channelled grooves of fluting) decorating table and chair legs, etc. in the late Georgian Period.

*Rococo*  From the French *rocaille*, rockwork; the decoration of 'C'- and 'S'-scrolls, often asymmetrical, which succeeded the baroque. The English version of rococo furniture is presented in Chippendale's *Director* (1754).

*Romayne*  Profile heads in medallions carved on early Tudor furniture and panels in attempted imitation of Italian Renaissance decoration.

*Seaweed marquetry*  A modern term for the intricate form of arabesque marquetry found on late Stuart furniture.

*Shell (coquillage)*  Popular motif of the early eighteenth century, especially on the knees of cabriole legs. Also found in rococo decoration and as the cresting of seats in the Adam Period.

*Splat*   The vertical member of a chair back, stretching from the rear seat rail to the cresting, as an essential part of the curvilinear chair.

*Split baluster*   A turned member split centrally to form two matching halves and then applied to the surface of furniture.

*Stile*   The vertical member connecting with the rail (q.v.).

*Strapwork*   The geometrical and arabesque ornament, closely interlaced, on late Tudor furniture: of Flemish origin.

*Stretcher*   The bar joining and bracing the legs of tables, chairs etc., normally horizontal but also of serpentine form in the late seventeenth century.

*Stringing*   Fine lines of inlaid wood or brass on late Georgian furniture.

*Tambour*   The roll front of desks, etc., made up of narrow strips of wood on canvas, of the late Georgian Period.

*Tenon*   See MORTISE.

*Tester*   The wooden canopy of a bedstead supported by a headboard and two end posts, or by four posts.

*Through dovetail*   One that passes through the wood exposing the end-grain on two surfaces; cf. the lapped or stopped dovetail which does not go through the wood but is concealed at one side.

*Vitruvial scroll*   The 'wave' pattern of scrolls, of classical origin, used as a decoration on furniture, especially on the friezes of side tables in the Kent Period.

# Selected Book List

The following is a useful selection of books on antique English furniture divided into general works, detailed studies, furniture designs and booklets; periodicals are listed separately.

GENERAL WORKS

*The Dictionary of English Furniture*, P. Macquoid and R. Edwards, 1954, 3 vols.
*The Shorter Dictionary of English Furniture*, R. Edwards, 1964
*A Short Dictionary of Furniture*, J. Gloag, 1969
*English Furniture Styles from 1500 to 1830*, R. Festnedge, 1960
*The Country Life Book of English Furniture*, E. T. Joy, 1968
*World Furniture*, ed. H. Hayward, 1970
*English Furniture*, J. C. Rogers, 1959
*The Connoisseur Complete Period Guides*, 1968

DETAILED STUDIES

*Sheraton Furniture*, R. Fastnedge, 1962
*Adam, Hepplewhite and other Neo-Classical Furniture*, C. Musgrave, 1966
*Regency Furniture*, C. Musgrave, 1970
*19th Century English Furniture*, E. Aslin, 1962
*Furniture 700–1700*, E. Mercer, 1969
*Georgian Cabinet-Makers*, R. Edwards and M. Jourdain, 1955
*The Furniture of Robert Adam*, E. Harris, 1963
*Furniture Making in 17th and 18th Century England*, R. W. Symonds, 1955
*The Englishman's Chair*, J. Gloag, 1964

PATTERN BOOKS

Tiranti Reprints of designs by Chippendale, Sheraton, Hepplewhite, Manwaring, Shearer, Ince and Mayhew; also *Treatise of Japanning and Varnishing* by Stalker and Parker, 1688.
Dover Publications Reprints of Chippendale's *Director (1762)*, 1966, Hepplewhite's *Guide (1794)*, 1969, *Crystal Palace Illustrated Catalogue, /1851)*, 1970 and *Blackies Cabinet Maker's Assistant (1853)*, 1970.
*Regency Furniture Designs*, ed. J. Harris, 1961

*English Furniture Designs of the 18th Century*, P. Ward-Jackson, 1958

BOOKLETS

From Victoria and Albert Museum
  *English Cabinets*, 1964
  *Chests of Drawers and Commodes*, 1960
  *Tables*, 1968
  *English Desks and Bureaux*, 1968
  *English Chairs*, 1970
*101 Chairs*, ed. P. Agius, 1970 (Greenhill House, Adderbury, Oxon)

PERIODICALS

*The Connoisseur*          *Apollo*
*Country Life*             *Burlington Magazine*
*Antique Collector*        *Collectors' Guide*
*Antiques (U.S.A.)*        *Art and Antiques Weekly*